This book is dedicated to the memory of Rose Kozak, my mother, a restless spirit determined to finish any task that she set upon. At times, she would plunge in without much thought or fear of the consequences. Rose was, however, an introspective person. She questioned her motives, many times thinking that perhaps there was a better way. But once she made up her mind, there was no stopping her. Thank God her intuitions proved to be more right than wrong. Without her courage, determination, and strong faith, our escape from Communist Czechoslovakia in October of 1949, and subsequent journey to the United States, would not have happened.

She adhered to one axiom: "Yes, I can."
John Kozak

Acknowledgments

My first eighty-page draft was given to my wife's cousin, Caroline "Boots" Morisette, for a quick overview. Caroline found it interesting and passed it on to her best friend, Peggy Shine, who is the daughter of Neal Shine, the former editor and publisher of the *Detroit Free Press*. Peggy apparently felt that my story had merit and gave it to her father to read. Neal took time from his busy schedule to meet with me a number of times. He edited many chapters, wrote the back cover synopsis, suggested I write in more narrative, and encouraged me to expand my story. Without Neal's help, I probably would have stopped at page eighty. As a result, I probed deeper into my mother's notes, letters, and partially written stories, which were given to me upon her passing.

My sister, Zdenka Sellenraad, deserves a multitude of praise. She was an unwitting source of information, providing me with memories long forgotten, and she helped fill in many blanks. Without Zdenka's help and courage, my mother may not have been able to formulate our escape.

Patricia McDonald, O.P., Ed. D., a Dominican Sister of Adrian and author of several books, critiqued my manuscript and encouraged me to publish it soon so the audience who experienced those years, 1942–1987, may enjoy reading it.

JJ Benkert, my sister-in-law, suggested more personal descriptions of the people in the story, their feelings, the type of clothes they wore, and how they intermingled with one another.

My daughter, Cynthia Kozak, graduated from Champlain College in Burlington, Vermont, on December 12, 2006, with an English and Creative Writing major. She took it upon herself to do additional editing of my story, and although it has been critiqued several times, she still found ways to make it better. Her associate, Scott André Campbell, drew maps and retouched photos that support my mother's story.

Last but not least, the confidence my wife Michelle had that I would finish my story encouraged me to keep writing.

Preface

My mother started writing her story years ago. She did not have a formal education but was so passionate about writing this story that she enrolled in a night school creative writing class. She developed congestive heart failure later in life and mentioned to me that she wished for her story to be finished in the event her heart failed. Rose passed away in 1992 at age eighty-five. Her story was unfinished, and I was left with a guilty conscience. After twelve years of procrastinating, I decided to finish it out of deference to her. The main events are true; however, some of the names, descriptions, exact circumstances, and my mother's thoughts, are suppositions based on what I believe happened. I wrote this story the way Rose would have enjoyed reading it; a validation of her bravery that culminated into a successful life for her family in the United States.

Chapter 1

The world cares very little about what a
man or woman knows; it is what the man
or woman is able to do that counts.

--Booker T. Washington

Snow was falling, covering with its soft white mantle the stately villas of this thousand-year-old city steeped in the turbulent history of Central Europe. It was home to good King Wenceslaus; the Holy Roman Emperor Charles IV; Jan Huss, the reformation priest who challenged Rome; Jan Ziska, the charismatic reformation leader who defeated the Pope's Hapsburg armies; and composers such as Anton Dvorak and Bedrich Smetana, among many others.

Once again, Czech lands were invaded. Neville Chamberlain, the Prime Minister of England, capitulated to the demands of Adolf Hitler during the Munich Conference on September 29, 1938. Eduard Benes', the president of Czechoslovakia, was deemed inconsequential. German armies marched into Prague; the onslaught was sudden, the occupation deadly.

"Not to worry," was the prevailing wisdom of many wishful-thinking Czechs. "We are bound by treaty to England and France. They will come to our rescue."

A few weeks later, when the truth was known, that hope changed to a lament: "Where are you, oh heroes of old? Awake, knights of Blanik! Come out of your mountain and slay the enemy! Czech lands are invaded! Our allies

1

have abandoned us!" Ancient legend told of St. Wenceslaus, asleep in the mountain called Blanik, with his army of knights. They would emerge during times of danger to the motherland and slay the invading armies. At this time, however, Blanik, surrounded by rolling meadows and fields brimming with wild flowers, stood remotely silent.

It was 3:00 AM, and the air was bitter cold. Rose opened her eyes to the soft ringing of an alarm clock. She reached across the night table and quickly shut it off, lest she wake Anthony, her husband. Her sleep was fitful in anticipation of the journey ahead. Rose pulled back the feather thick and quietly climbed out of her warm bed, onto the cold hardwood floor. Warmth from their tiled heating unit standing in the corner of their bedroom diminished hours before. Frost crystallized on the windows, and her breath was visible in the cold room. Anthony did not have to get up for another three hours, and there was nothing else she wanted to say to him. The decision was made the night before. They were running out of food. Rose wanted to go, but Anthony felt that it was his duty as the head of the household. He was a proud man.

"Tomorrow I will leave early in the morning and travel to the farm we know near Kolin," Anthony said to Rose the night before. "I am certain I will return with a chicken or at least some cheese and potatoes."

"Anthony, you will be missed at work," Rose countered. "I know you feel that it's too dangerous for me, but I went several times before and nothing happened. I will arouse less suspicion in case they stop me."

Anthony continued to protest but knew she was right. If he was caught, he would be shot, and there would be no income for the family. However, if Rose was caught, there may be clemency shown towards a woman.

Rose knew she must hurry to catch the 5:15 AM train out of Prague. She stepped out of her warm flannel nightgown and dressed quickly in the darkness, remembering where she laid her clothes the night before. She carefully packed the five sweaters she knitted into a large rucksack. The sweaters were to be used as barter for food—perhaps a dozen eggs, a duck, or a chicken—from a sympathetic farmer. This food would provide enough nourishment to supplement her family's meager diet for several weeks.

The date was February 8, 1945, during the waning days of the Nazi occupation of Bohemia and Moravia, the western portion of a divided Czechoslovakia. Slovakia, the eastern portion, received favored status by the Nazis because they promised not to resist the invaders. Food was scarce, and what there was went first to the German army.

Anthony, Rose's husband, was a manager at Czecho-Slavia, the largest freight-forwarding company in Czechoslovakia. He was a forwarder by occupation, an expert in the business of importing and exporting products from one country to another. He was fluent in eight languages and did his best to provide for his family. Food was strictly rationed, and with a three-year-old son, a thirteen-year-old daughter, and two grandparents in the same household, there was never enough.

This was Rose's third trip to the countryside. It never seemed to get easier or less dangerous. The Nazis continually watched trains and buses for any type of contraband or food smuggling. Security was tight following the assassination of Reinhardt Heydrich, the Butcher of Prague, and the bloody reprisal on Lidice, a village northwest of Prague, which was completely destroyed—all males over fourteen were killed. Now no Czech was above suspicion.

Rose pulled on her fur-lined leather boots, slipped her arms into her heavy, dark brown wool coat, and wrapped a thick wool shawl, which her mother had knitted, around her head and neck. She slipped on her gloves and strapped the rucksack onto her back. Before walking out, she peeked into her children's bedroom. Both Zdenka and Jaroslav were sleeping soundly, oblivious to the problems of the world. *How comforting*, thought Rose, *to have someone else take care of you; the blissful innocence of youth.*

She quietly slipped out the front door, into the snow-filled darkness, pulling the heavy wooden door shut behind her, careful to not wake anyone. The cold wind numbed her face. She tightened the shawl around her neck, pulling it up over her mouth to keep the wind from scoring her face. With each step, the blowing snow covered her footprints … gone without a trace. *I'm a ghost*, she thought, looking back. *Is life this ephemeral?* she wondered. Rose walked along the snow-covered path, between the two tall linden trees standing like giant sentinels on each side of the path. She walked up several stone steps and pushed open the creaking wrought iron gate to the sidewalk in front of her home. She turned to her right, walked another thirty feet, and descended a stone staircase along the east side of their property. The stone staircase was a shortcut between the houses; it led down to a main street, which wound its way towards downtown Prague and the train station near Wenceslaus square.

The old cobblestone steps were uneven and blanketed with snow, making them slippery. Rose stepped gingerly in the darkness, trying to not lose her balance, her breath visible through her scarf. When she reached the main street below, her pace picked up.

As her boots crunched through the snow, she reflected on her fifteen years of marriage to Anthony; the birth of their son, Jaroslav, on February 6, 1942, during the darkest days of the occupation; and the birth of their daughter, Zdenka, ten years earlier in Bratislava, the capital and largest city of Slovakia. It was a former coronation city of Hungarian kings, with a prominent castle on the top of a hill overlooking the Danube River, providing protection from invading tribes during the days of old. It was a historical city, where Rose and Anthony married on December 20, 1930.

It was also the place where Rose suffered a misfortune she would have liked to forget. Several years before the war started, Anthony, fearing the depreciation of Czech currency, exchanged a large portion of their nest egg for two diamond necklaces. He asked Rose to take care of them while he traveled to Prague to assume his new position as a director of Czecho-Slavia and to find a home for his family and his aging parents. Rose wore the diamonds around her neck, under a high collar, for safe keeping. At night, she always placed them on the night table next to her bed. However, by the time Anthony found the home and asked Rose, Zdenka, and his parents to join him, one of the necklaces disappeared. Suspicion pointed to Maria the cleaning lady, who came twice a week. Rose remembered the morning Maria was cleaning the bedroom and noticed them laying on the night table. She commented to Rose, "Mrs. Kozak, those necklaces look beautiful. Are they real diamonds?"

"No, they are not," Rose remembered answering, in an effort to dispel further interest. "They are imitations." The following day, Rose noticed one missing. She searched everywhere but could not find it. Maria did not come to work. Rose called the police, but when they looked for Maria her apartment was empty and she had disappeared. Although the impending war made this incident small in scope, Rose felt responsible and vowed to redeem herself.

She remembered how Anthony was reluctant to propose marriage, even after graduating from the Consular Academy in Vienna, Austria, because his position was not secured. *How silly*, she thought. Just then, her daydream was cut short.

A spotlight shined on her face, and a commanding voice asked in German, "Where are you going, madam?"

She was so engrossed in her thoughts she didn't notice the black Mercedes sedan quietly pulling up alongside her in the driving snow, like a panther stalking its prey. The car headlights were turned off, and the spotlight blinded her momentarily, catching her by surprise. She raised her hand over her eyes to cut the glare.

Gestapo! Her mind shrieked, sending shivers down her back. To be caught walking, alone at this time of the night, in an occupied city abounding with resistance activities, was reason enough to be stopped and have your identification papers checked. Even now, so close to the end of the war, the Gestapo were feared for their systematic efforts to eliminate any evidence of their brutalities from the advancing allies. They were Hitler's secret police, known for their skillful ability to make people disappear.

"Your papers, please!" was the next command. Rose felt disoriented but squelched her fear, knowing they preyed on weakness. She pulled off her gloves, reached into her coat pocket, took out her identification papers, and placed them in the black-gloved hand that reached out of the car window.

"And where are you going so early in the morning?" the voice asked again, with an edge.

"I'm taking the early train to Kolin to visit my sick aunt," Rose lied, adding, "I am a Czech citizen but also an American," hoping it would make a difference.

It did; the voice became more conciliatory. "I have an uncle in the textile business in Charlotte, North Carolina. Perhaps after the war, when we have defeated the Bolsheviks with our American friends, I will visit him."

Rose was surprised that they actually believed the wild rumors circulating through the German Army that the Americans would soon align themselves with the Germans, against the Russians. However, she wasn't surprised by the changed tone. She speculated from the British Broadcasting Company radio messages, which Anthony and many other Czechs listened to each night, that in another few weeks, these Nazi henchmen would throw away their incriminating uniforms and run to the American zone, pleading their innocence.

"We were soldiers just following orders," would be their mantra. They knew they didn't stand a chance at clemency from the Russians, not after the devastation their invasion caused in Leningrad, Moscow, Stalingrad, etc.

"What is in your rucksack, please?" he asked pointing to her shoulders.

"Sweaters and clothing for my aunt," replied Rose.

The car door opened, and a tall man with dark glasses, dressed in black, stepped out. He had on a black hat, black leather coat, black boots, and black leather gloves. There was an air of dominance about him as he stood under the streetlight in the blowing snow, like something out of a Gothic novel. Rose bit the inside of her lip, resolute to look brave.

"Turn around so I can check your rucksack!" he barked. Rose did as she was told. He took off his black gloves, took out his flashlight, and rummaged through her rucksack. "How many sweaters does your aunt need?" he asked sarcastically. "Is this barter for food, perhaps?"

"No, of course not!" stammered Rose. "My aunt is old and sick; she needs warm clothing. We have a severe winter. I'm not breaking any of your laws. Please let me go; otherwise, I'll miss my train." She tried her best to sound convincing.

"Is your husband also an American?" he asked, surprising her with this question

"No, he is Czech," Rose replied, realizing that she was being set up. Had she said that Anthony was an American, they would have surmised that he was a diplomat and wondered why she was not chauffeured, creating additional suspicion as to where she was going this early in the morning.

"Where is he?" he asked impatiently.

"My husband is a director at Czecho-Slavia," she replied. "He will be getting up shortly for work, where he is needed to decipher export tariffs between our two countries; otherwise, he would have accompanied me."

"There are no two countries anymore. What was Czechoslovakia is now part of the Third Reich!" he shouted. "Is Czecho-Slavia the forwarding company on Wenceslaus Square?" he asked.

"Yes it is," Rose answered, wondering why he was asking all these questions.

"Be careful, madam," he warned, handing back her identification. "Because of partisan activities by your compatriots, our laws are severe and must be obeyed! Being an American will not save you." He climbed back into his car.

The Mercedes slowly disappeared into the snowy night, a stalker preying on the weak and unsuspecting. It took Rose several minutes to calm down; cold sweat ran down her back. In spite of her warm clothing, she shivered. She walked faster now, trying to make up for lost time. The exercise calmed her, and she resumed thinking about her courtship to Anthony.

It began as a whirlwind romance during her first trip to Europe in 1924. She was visiting relatives and learning European culture. A soul-stirring glance and the returned smile sparked a budding romance, which, after three years, blossomed into a serious relationship. By then, Rose hoped for a wedding proposal or at least an engagement ring before having to return home to Detroit, Michigan. Her parents, aware of her relationship with Anthony but worried that it was just a fling that wasn't going anywhere, asked her to return home. She remembered his reluctance to propose marriage and found it hard to understand his reasoning.

"My family would help us get started financially. They know how hard it is in the beginning and would be willing to help," she had pleaded with Anthony. "When my mother and father married, they received help from my mother's family." It was an acceptable practice for the family to help out their newlywed daughter; it was considered a part of her dowry. However it was time for her to abide by her parents wishes, return home, and become gainfully employed. She hoped Anthony would reconsider before she left.

Hearing this from his future bride, the woman with whom he planned to start a family and planned to support, only hurt Anthony's pride. "I suggest you return to the United States and wait for my letter," he replied testily. "It may take some time, perhaps a year or two, before I have a secured position with a good company that needs my skills. Only then will I be able to support you, and only then will I ask for your hand in marriage. In the meantime, I will write to you every week, expressing my deep feelings and the wonderful life we will enjoy after I have secured a proper position."

Rose was hurt, thinking, *that will be the day, when I have to wait a year or two for a formal marriage proposal!* She remembered returning to the United States in a huff, feeling forlorn and hurt, not realizing how serious Anthony was and how much he loved her. Yet she knew that until his position was secured, he would not be able to care for her in the way that was expected of him. It was the European way. Nevertheless, she pouted.

A faint train whistle through the howling wind cut into her thoughts, making her aware of the proximity of the train station. "Perhaps another mile or two," she estimated. She kept up her brisk pace, crossing the Charles Bridge which spanned the Vltava River. The statues of saints that adorned both sides of the bridge shimmered like ghosts in the dim streetlight, which penetrated through the swirling snow. They had a calming effect on Rose, reassuring her that she was not alone. Feeling confident, she returned to her bittersweet memories.

She remembered returning to her parent's home in Highland Park, Michigan, a suburb of Detroit, in 1927. She worked as a secretary at the Frigidaire Corporation in Detroit, and took night classes at the Detroit Business Institute. She was twenty years old, and she had a conversational command of two foreign languages and felt more mature than before she left. She was determined not to repeat the folly of her teenage years, which she felt was the reason her parents sent her to Europe. She quickened her pace and reflected on those painful years.

Chapter 2

No coward soul is mine,
No trembler in the world's storm-troubled sphere,
I see heaven's glories shine,
And faith shines equal, arming me from fear.

--Emily Bronte

Her mind drifted back to 1922, when she was fifteen, in the tenth grade, and played as a forward on the girls' high school basketball team in Saginaw, Michigan, where they lived at that time. She remembered her parent's reaction.

"Young ladies do not play men's sports. Basketball is a man's sport!" her father said. "You should learn to play the piano instead!"

"Why don't you study home economics like I did?" her mother suggested. "Sewing, knitting, and cooking will teach you to take care of the home you will have someday."

Rose wanted to play and sneaked off to basketball practice just the same. Jimmy, her brother, and Josephine, her sister, made up excuses for her to their parents, telling them that Rose was tutoring other children after school.

Rose scored many points and became the captain of the girl's basketball team. Because of her efforts, they won many games, including their last game of the season.

One evening she came home at 8:00 PM, two hours after dinner. It was dark outside, and after four days of coming home late, her parents had found out that she played basketball against their wishes. She was sent to bed without supper. Josephine and Jimmy felt sorry for her, knowing how she loved the game and how hard she played.

Rose rushed downstairs the next morning to look at the Saturday paper before her father got to it. She took the sports section upstairs to her bedroom and showed it to her sister and brother. A paragraph under "High School Basketball" showed that Rose Kousak scored twenty-two points, more than anyone else, and led her team to a district championship. Later that day, Josephine and Jimmy showed the paper to their mother. She remembered how they stuck up for her and was proud to be their older sister.

"Mother, you and dad should be proud of Rose. She played very hard and everyone at school thinks she is great!" Josephine shouted excitedly. "The entire girl's basketball team was praised by the principal, thanks to Rose. She's a heroine at school, yet you punish her at home. It just doesn't seem fair. She played her heart out."

"She disobeyed us!" snapped Hedwig, not used to be being reprimanded by her daughter. Rose remembered how her mother's bark was always worse than her bite and how surprised and delighted she was by Josephine's defense of her sister. *It's the way it should be,* Hedwig thought, *sisters sticking up for each other.* Feeling a little remorseful after Josephine's outburst, she said, "Perhaps you are right. Your father and I may have been too strict. We should learn more about how girls play sports in this country." She later showed the paper to her husband, saying, "We may have a headstrong daughter, but you must admit she is a champion."

Rose remembered being summoned by her father to his den and his solemn voice when he said, "I do not like being disobeyed; on the other hand, I must complement you on your victory. I admit that I know little about girls' basketball or how schools encourage women to play sports in this country." Rose remembered walking on a cloud; that's all she needed to hear—that her father was proud of her.

Her thoughts were interrupted by an escalating noise from heavy motor vehicles. Several armored cars drove by, alerting her of increased German activity. She remembered from her past trips that security was always tight around the train station. The Germans were constantly watching for acts of sabotage. Her vigilance increased. She made a cursory check for her identification papers in case she was stopped again. Finding everything in order, she tucked them back into the deep recess of her pocket and once again checked her watch. It was 4:30 AM, still plenty of time to make the train. She resumed thinking back to those sweet but troublesome teenage years, back to 1923, when she was sixteen.

She was an attractive, well-developed young woman, who turned the heads of many men. She remembered the summer she had a job at a local drug store soda fountain, serving cherry Cokes and malted milkshakes. A handsome young man, who drove a shiny new convertible, frequently stopped for lunch. He always asked for her and normally ordered a Coke and a sandwich. Her girlfriends said his name was Boyd and that he had a good job. He had a friendly smile and was very popular with all the girls. One day, while sitting at the soda fountain, he looked at Rose and, with a smile, asked, "Wouldn't you like to go for a ride in my convertible?"

Rose was surprised but said, "No thanks."

Her girlfriends who worked with her could not believe that she turned him down. "He is so cute. What is wrong with you? What are you afraid of? He's so friendly."

She laughed at them but deep inside felt excited that an older man found her attractive. She heard he was twenty and worked in his father's business.

Boyd persisted, "I'll have you home in plenty of time for dinner."

"I am sorry, but my answer is still no," Rose replied.

The following day she left work early, and as she was walking home, Boyd pulled up in his convertible. In his friendly voice, he said, "Jump in, Rose. We can go for a short ride. I promise to have you home in time for dinner." It was a sunny afternoon, and Rose decided, *what the heck? He's friendly. What harm can come of it?* She jumped in. He drove fast, and the wind felt great in her hair. It was the first time she was out alone with a young man. She knew all the girls were crazy about Boyd and felt giddy that he picked her over them. They drove out into the country, laughing and joking. All of a sudden, he turned off the paved road and drove down a dirt trail and into a cornfield. He shut the motor off and reached across to Rose. Astonished and frightened, she remembered pulling away and the assault that followed.

"What are you doing?" she asked anxiously. He grabbed her arm. "Let me go," she said, trying to twist away from him. "Take your hands off me, and take me home right now!" she demanded.

"Don't be a fool. Why do you suppose I took you for a ride?" he replied, putting his arms around her. He pushed his hot face against her neck, trying to hold her down.

"Let go of me," she cried, punching him in the face. He tried to reach up her dress. With a wild cry, Rose twisted sideways, kneed him in the groin, and stuck her thumb in his eye. He screamed and loosened his grip. She opened the door and jumped out of the car. Sobbing, she ran out of the cornfield, onto the main road.

A few minutes later, his car pulled up next to her. "Come on, Rose. I'm sorry. Please climb in," he pleaded through the open window. "I'll take you home. You know, I can hardly see out of my left eye." He was hoping for a little sympathy but got none.

"That's too bad!" Rose hissed. "You deserved it!"

"I didn't mean any harm. I thought you wanted to have some fun. Please jump in."

"No, I'm walking home," Rose snapped.

It was getting dark. She remembered how frightened she was. They were miles from her home. *What will my parents say about me coming home so late?* She wondered.

Boyd got out of the car and ran after her, pleading, "Look, I lost my head. I'm sorry; please let me take you home." She climbed into his car without a word. They drove in silence.

Hedwig and James were waiting on the front porch, worried because Rose did not come home for dinner. When Boyd and Rose pulled up, James walked up to the car, looked into Boyd's eyes, and angrily demanded, "Who are you? How dare you take my daughter for a ride without asking my permission?"

Boyd was at a loss for words. He wanted to apologize but was afraid that James would punch him. Rose jumped out of the car, tears running down her face.

She ran into her house, ran up to her bedroom, took off her clothes, climbed into bed, buried her head in the pillow, and wept. Josephine, her younger sister, who slept in the same room, woke up and asked, "What happened?"

"Nothing," cried Rose, "He tried but I stopped him."

She cried herself to sleep. Later that night, she awoke to a noise and saw her mother come in and check her undergarments. *They don't trust me,* she anguished and whimpered back to sleep. Rose remembered how upset her parents were and how she vowed not to let that happen again.

Several weeks had passed after that incident and life seemed to have returned to normal, or so Rose thought. Her father was still distraught over his first-born turning into an attractive young lady who seemed naïve about the ways of men. He discussed his feelings with his wife, who advised patience, stating, "All normal young ladies her age are interested in young men. Rose is a mature young woman who knows how to handle herself. We raised her well. Please stop worrying."

James Kousak did not stop worrying. He felt the morals of the country were decaying. "There appears to be a lack of respect by young people towards their elders; it's not like when we were their age," he replied.

Hedwig laughed, saying, "Did you forget when we left Kutina the first time? It was against my parents wishes."

"That may be so, but I always respected them," he grumbled.

"Rose loves you and respects you, but she's a teenager, and being interested in boys is normal," Hedwig replied.

Rose continued her part-time job at the local drug store, working behind the soda fountain with her friend Dorothy Batson. One day, around noon, two well-dressed young men walked in, sat down at the counter, and ordered lunch. The tallest was over six feet and had blond hair and a friendly smile. The other one stood a little shorter, was stockier, and had dark hair with a pencil mustache. Both wore vested suits. They noticed the girls and engaged them in a friendly conversation while they ate. When they finished, the tall one asked Rose, "Would you two young ladies like to go on a double date tonight?" Both Rose and Dorothy were caught by surprise. To be noticed by these two successful-looking men was a heady experience.

Dorothy was excited and whispered to Rose, "Shall we go?"

Rose hesitated, remembering her problem with Boyd not so long ago. She had an idea that if they stopped by her house and introduced themselves to her parents, everything would work out well. They were well dressed and mannerly. Why shouldn't her parents like them?

"If you want me to join you on a double date, you will have to ask my parents for permission," she said, hoping not to sound childish

They laughed, thinking it was a strange request but when Dorothy, in support of her friend and not wishing to go alone, said, "I'll only come if Rose's father lets her." They agreed to visit with Rose's parents and ask their permission. Rose gave the tall one her address and told him, "We get off by six tonight."

"Good. We'll pick you up at your house."

After work, Rose and Dorothy anxiously walked to Rose's home in anticipation of her father's permission and a fun night out.

As soon as Rose walked through the door and saw her mother's worried look, she knew something was wrong. Her father, in a rage, walked up to her, slapped her across the face, and yelled, "What kind of a fool do you take me for, asking a married man to seek my permission to date you? That man is a married twenty-two-year-old whose wife just had a baby! He works at Chrysler near my department and didn't recognize me until I told him who I was and where I worked. He mumbled an apology and ran out the door; his friend ran after him." Noticing Dorothy, he directed his anger at both of them, asking, "What's wrong with you girls? Where are your morals, going out with married men?"

By then, Dorothy was out the door, frightened out of her wits. Rose remembered how stunned she was. Her father never struck her before. She could not believe what just happened and what she heard. She wiped the blood from her lips, and cried out defensively, "I didn't know he was married. I just wanted to do what I thought was right and have him ask for your permission. I'm sorry!" She ran up to her room, flopped on her bed, and cried into her pillow. She heard her parents arguing downstairs.

A short time later, her mother came into her room and sat on the bed beside her. She stroked her head and, in a calm voice, said, "Your father loves you very much. He watched you grow into a beautiful young lady and would like to protect you forever but knows that he cannot. "

"Then he should learn to trust me," Rose squeaked, gasping for air and wiping her nose.

"Yes, he should," her mother replied, "but remember, he is European, and over there, young ladies didn't have the freedom they have here. Young men did not approach ladies unless they were properly introduced first."

That was all well and good, thought Rose, *but to be hit by your father for trying to do the right thing is unforgivable.* She remembered her decision to run away. The next day, she took forty dollars, which she had saved, out of her dresser drawer, packed a small suitcase, and walked out of the house as if going to school, but instead took a bus to Saginaw, Michigan. Upon arrival, she checked into a nearby YWCA, where she was introduced to a young woman named Carol with whom she was asked to share a room.

"Carol, what brought you to Saginaw?" Rose asked inquisitively.

"I ran away from home," Carol replied. "My parents wanted me to marry a widowed farmer, who I did not love and who was twenty-five years older than me.

"Why are you here?" Carol asked.

"My parents don't trust me," Rose replied, choking up. "I tried to do what I believed was proper, but instead of listening to me, my father struck me across my face! I decided to run away and hope to get a job and start a new life here."

"Me, too," replied Carol.

The next day, they both went their separate ways to look for a job. Within an hour, Rose found a job at a drug store soda fountain not far from the YWCA. No sooner did she start to work when she was called into the manager's office. To her surprise, she saw her mother sitting there with a troubled look on her face. "Mother!" Rose cried, astonished. "How did you find me?"

Before she could reply, the manager angrily asked, "Did you run away from home? I do not hire runaways!" He looked at Hedwig and imploringly said, "I did not know that she," he pointed at Rose, "ran away from home."

Hedwig ignored him and, in a grieving voice, said to Rose, "Your father and I love you very much and want you to come home."

Rose felt very remorseful. She rushed to her mother, wrapped her arms around her neck, and pleadingly asked, "I'm so sorry, Mother. Please forgive me. I want to come home; please take me home." Hand in hand, they walked to the YWCA, packed Rose's suitcase, and took the bus back to Highland Park. Before leaving, Rose left a note for Carol that she was returning home and hoped Carol would reconcile her differences with her parents and return also.

When Rose and her mother walked up the steps to her house, she wondered, with mounting fear, what her father would say. Her father was waiting for her in the hallway. Rose saw the crushed look on his face and knew, with relief, that he loved her and that all was forgiven. Rose loved her parents very much but knew she was growing up and hoped her father would be more understanding. She needed independence and wanted their trust.

Both her parents became aware of the changing morals in the United States. Young girls bobbed their hair, wore lipstick, and danced fast. Although it was prohibition, young men were known to carry flasks with alcohol to high school events. The times were changing, and this worried Hedwig and James. They worried about Rose, who showed a streak of troubling independence, and decided it was time for her to visit relatives in Europe and learn traditional values.

Chapter 3

When people are put into position,
Slightly above what they would expect,
They're apt to excel.

--Richard Branson

As Rose neared the train station, the wind increased, and the blowing snow obscured her vision. She stopped, wiped her eyes, and noticed the faint lights from the station. *Another quarter mile or so before I'm there*, she thought. She pulled her shawl over her nose to ward off the wind, and thought back, remembering how sad she felt when her parents summoned her home from that first trip to Europe.

She remembered wanting to stay longer, but her relatives, with whom she stayed, felt responsible for her and worried over her frequent trips to Vienna, where she visited with Anthony. They communicated their fears to her parents, who decided that they had spent enough money on her. She had spent three years frolicking in Europe with a man they had only heard about. Not hearing of any commitment worried them. Rose was confident that with a little more time, Anthony would have proposed marriage. Now she was forced to return empty handed. On the other hand, she would not have traded her experience for anything. In spite of her fears of the unknown, it was exciting to travel solo to Europe at age seventeen, just after graduating from high school; to be able to meet with representatives of Florence Ziegfeld on the boat and be asked to join the Follies, and to enjoy a Viennese opera, where she met Anthony. She felt exhilarated just thinking about it all. Her only regret was not receiving a wedding proposal, not even a darn engagement ring! Wise in the ways of men by age twenty, she was careful of whom she dated. Each week, she received letters from Anthony describing his feelings for her, hoping she still felt the same way towards him. Rose loved Anthony, but when he refused to propose marriage and suggested waiting until his position was secured, she remembered how hurt she was and how she questioned his sincerity.

What a bunch of baloney! She thought. *He just wants to keep me on a string while he plays the field. Well, two can play that game.*

She resumed an active life trying to forget Anthony. She dated a number of bachelors, one of whom was a successful lawyer named Ross. They dated for several months and grew quite fond of each other. However, Anthony's letters kept coming, becoming more frequent, with news of a wonderful opportunity in management with the Danube Navigation Company. He hoped she would join him soon, writing:

Rose, I am lost without you. My life is empty. I love you and am now in a position to support you. Please come.

She remembered receiving a letter from Julia, Anthony's mother, stating that Anthony was so despondent over her absence that he was falling into ill health and that if she didn't come soon, he would "jump into a well." She laughed, thinking, *so now he recruited his mother trying to coax me back.* In spite of how funny it all seemed, it played havoc with her emotions. By now, she believed his sincerity but was still hurt over returning home without an engagement ring.

She thought back to the evening when Ross proposed marriage. She was in a quandary, wondering what she should do. She had known it would eventually come to that and felt guilty not telling Ross about Anthony, feeling she led him on. *What to do?* she thought. Ross was destined to be a successful partner in his father's law firm. On the other hand, Anthony's letters were so poetically written, so full of hope, promising a wonderful future in Europe. She remembered the long walks they took in the Viennese woods, the sounds of the Strauss waltzes they listened and danced to, and all that wonderful history surrounding them. It was so romantic and exciting. She thought of life in Detroit, as the wife of an enterprising lawyer, raising children in a beautiful home in Palmer Park, near Ross's parents. She knew her parents would approve. They liked Ross and knew Rose would have a secure life with him. But something was missing. There was no excitement, no firecrackers, and no Roman candles bursting in the air like they did with Anthony in Vienna. It seemed dull! She considered all those fine points against traveling back to Europe, to uncertainty, to not knowing what the future held, not knowing any of the languages very well. But she knew that Anthony loved her and finally had his position. However, she received a letter from Anthony that almost changed her mind. He asked how much her dowry was so that he may furnish their apartment when they got married. Furiously, she flashed back a letter telling him, "I am not for sale," and in the heat of the moment, wrote, "I decided to marry someone who loves me for who I am and not how much I am worth!"

When her mother heard what she did, she explained that it was the custom in Europe for a man to expect a dowry from his future wife and that it should not be an obstacle to marriage. Then Rose's mother received a letter written in German from Anthony's mother, condemning Rose for leading her son on only to make him suffer the consequences of his love for her. When her mother translated the letter to Rose, she was aghast. *It was not like that at all,* she thought. She really loved him and realized she completely misunderstood his motive. She waited for three years and now knew the answer. With her mind made up, she quickly telegraphed Anthony: *I'm coming!*

She remembered the euphoria she felt: *Free at last, back to Europe and a new life.*

Rose was a good walker. She was pleased with herself, evading the Gestapo, walking more than an hour and a half in the snow-filled darkness with little physical discomfort, and still beating the train by thirty minutes.

Her jubilation was cut short. Several German personal carriers were parked in front of the train station. Minutes later, German soldiers pulled a struggling man out of the main door, dragged him down the steps, and shoved him into a black Mercedes waiting at the curb. Rose rested on a bench, slightly out of breath, and watched another sad debacle unfold. *How unfortunate,* she thought. He probably had a family and was caught smuggling contraband in his effort to feed them. She stymied her spreading fear and forced herself to think of happier times.

She thought of the time she first met Anthony at the Vienna National Opera, where she and Aunt Eva enjoyed Puccini's *La Boehme.* He was seated two rows behind them and was awestruck by Rose's beauty. He was in a dilemma as to how to approach her. After the opera, knowing it was improper for a stranger to directly introduce himself to a lady, he purchased two red roses from a young flower merchant.

"Young man," Anthony addressed the flower merchant, "see those two ladies?" he asked, pointing to Rose and her aunt as they walked out of the opera house.

"Yes?" replied the boy, wondering what this was all about.

"I want you to give a rose to each one. Here is a shilling for the good job you are going to do."

"Thank you," quipped the boy, pocketing his tip, intrigued by what promised to be an interesting situation.

As Rose and Aunt Eva came out of the theater, the young man approached with a smile, saying "Flowers for the ladies." He handed each a rose.

"Where did these come from?" Aunt Eva asked surprised.

"From him," said the boy, pointing to Anthony.

Anthony, dressed in a herringbone vested suit and tie, saw his opportunity. He politely tipped his hat, bowed, and approached Aunt Eva.

"Good evening, madam" he said. "May I have your permission to speak to the young lady?" He smiled at Rose.

Aunt Eva looked him over with suspicion and raised her umbrella in a threatening gesture, her icy voice cutting the evening air with a resounding, "No!" deflating Anthony's high expectations. "You are an impudent puppy! How dare you approach us in such a cavalier manner? Have you no shame?" she shouted.

"Madam, please, my intentions are honorable," Anthony replied, not to be denied. "Allow me to explain. I come from a good Christian family and am a student in my senior year at the Consular Academy here in Vienna, studying international tariffs. Upon graduation, a position, hopefully, will be available for me with the Danube Navigation Company."

Aunt Eva, a five foot seven inch, 220-pound, pugnacious woman, was not impressed; she did, however, have a soft heart and, noticing his courteous manner and dress, said, "Only if the lady allows it." Rose, her curiosity piqued, smiled at Anthony and nodded in agreement.

"Just for a minute and no touching!" thundered Aunt Eva. "I am walking right behind you!" She walked a few steps behind them, listening to every word. She had her umbrella clenched tightly in her hand, ready to thump Anthony on the head lest he make an improper gesture.

How wonderful it all was, Rose thought, as she watched for the train. She hoped it would be her last trip. She knew the Allies were approaching. She just didn't know how soon.

Anthony's radio, kept hidden in the fireplace, was replete with news about the approach of the Allies. Every few days, around 11:00 PM, after Jaroslav and Zdenka went to bed, Anthony listened to the BBC. The stoic voice of Winston Churchill reassured his listeners that Allied armies were defeating the Germans on all fronts and that the end was in sight. Although Rose hoped the Americans would arrive first, she heard a deal had been struck between Eisenhower and Stalin, allowing the Russians to occupy Prague.

General Patton's army, which swept east across the southern part of Europe, was ordered to stop near the city of Plzen, a large industrial center seventy miles southwest of Prague. It was best known for the Skoda Engineering Works, which manufactured armaments, turbines, tractors, and locomotives necessary for supplying the Nazi war machine. It was a strategic target for the allies. With its capture by General Patton's Third Army, the Germans were cut off from a large source of supplies, and the war ended sooner.

Chapter 4

You turn if you want to. This lady's not for turning.

--Margaret Thatcher

The train station was a maelstrom of confusion. People were milling around, trying desperately to find the right train for their destination. Rose quickly purchased her ticket and walked out on the platform. Hissing steam from locomotives, a mass of humanity rubbing shoulder-to-shoulder, shrill whistles from conductors, the shriek of metal wheels moving on metal tracks, and the sharp snap of switches moving trains from one track to another echoed throughout the busy terminal. Rose felt lost. Although she had made this trip before, the complex was huge and trains were constantly redirected to serve the German Army.

"Which is the train for Kolin?" she asked a busy porter.

"Track sixteen, due to pull out in ten minutes. This is track five," he replied. "You must cross to the other platform, over there," he said, pointing to the far side of the terminal. "Hurry or you will miss it!"

"Thank you," she replied, running across the busy terminal with the heavy rucksack on her back. She found her train just as it was pulling out, grabbed the outstretched hand of a helpful conductor, and leaped aboard.

The sight of Nazi uniforms returned her to reality. A rescue was still far off. Prague was under German occupation, and her mission to bring food home to her family was of primary importance. The train was packed with Czechs hoping to find food in the countryside, and with German soldiers hoping to stay alive, knowing the end was near but still hoping for a miracle. Rose heard Anthony say, after listening to one of the Allies' broadcasts, that the Germans were told by their officers not to give up hope that Hitler had a secret weapon, which would turn the tide.

The air was filled with smoke, sweat, uncertainty, fear, and sadness. No one knew what the future would bring. They all hoped for the best but prepared to save themselves and their families any way they could. Rose was filled with an overwhelming dose of adrenalin, a strong spirit of adventure, and a single-minded determination to succeed. Her mindset overrode any fear she felt.

She pulled off her rucksack, sat down next to a window, placed the rucksack under her feet, and watched the dawn slowly breaking over the flat, snow-covered farmlands. She knew the train ride would take at least an hour and allowed her mind to drift back once more.

She remembered how proud Anthony was when he received news that his resume was well received and that he was hired by a reputable company. He became employed by the Danube Navigation Company, his first position since graduating from the Consular Academy. It was important for a young, educated man planning on marriage to have a position, a managerial job with a chance for advancement, so that he may provide for his wife and future family. This was expected by many European families at that time. Soon after their wedding, a better position became available with Czecho-Slavia, a large forwarding company that was looking for Anthony's talents. Over a few short years, Anthony advanced into upper management.

She thought about the time, a few months after their wedding, when she and Anthony decided to sunbathe just east of Vienna, along the northern bank of the Danube River. It was an unusually warm, windy June afternoon, and the sandy shore had wooden changing huts dotting the bank. There were other people sunbathing, but no one was in the water. Anthony and Rose changed into their bathing suits, walked out on the beach, and sat on their towel, enjoying the sunshine.

"It's such a hot day. Why don't we jump in and cool off?" Rose asked.

"Rose, the Danube flows from the Swiss Alps and will be very cold. It is still spring!" replied Anthony, surprised by her request. He hesitated to step into the river because he did not know how to swim, but thinking she just wanted to wade in the shallows and wanting to appear brave, he stood up and waded up to his waist, where the current was still weak. "Jump in if you wish, but I'm warning you, the water is cold!" He didn't think she would do it.

With a running start, Rose dove into the water. *I'll show him*, she thought gleefully. The water was mind-numbingly cold, and the current, to her surprise, swiftly pulled her out into the swirling midstream, flowing fast and deep. Feeling the strength of the current pulling her downstream, she turned to swim towards shore. She noticed Anthony frantically waving his arms, a helpless look on his face. Others gathered along the shore, looking on curiously, but nobody dared to jump into the cold current to help Rose. Determined, she struck out in a strong breaststroke, her favorite swimming style. When she looked above the waves to take a breath, she saw Anthony slowly fading away. Rose was a strong swimmer but realized the current was too strong to swim against. Her arms grew tired in the cold Alpine water. Gusting winds whipped the water into a white froth. Each time she raised her head to breathe, she swallowed water. She tried swimming at an angle with the current, towards shore, but just as she thought she was swimming out of it, the swift current near the high bank pulled her back out. Unable to catch her breath, she started to struggle, her lungs crying for oxygen, her legs growing numb.

Slow down, she told herself. *The current will beat you; use it to your advantage.* At that point, she gave up fighting, turned onto her back, and let herself be swept downstream, conserving energy, praying for an opportunity to swim out.

Anthony feared for Rose's life. He watched in disbelief that his new bride had the courage to dive into a swift, very cold river without any apparent concern for her own safety. He knew the river well, having traveled to the Black Sea and back to Vienna many times as a manager with the Danube Navigation Company before they were married. He knew the river was deep, with treacherous currents, and was unpredictable. What he didn't know, but soon found out, was that Rose was a strong swimmer who loved the water and was just as unpredictable as the Danube.

He dressed quickly, ran up the bank, hailed a taxi, and followed the river for four miles, watching Rose, a tiny speck in a wide body of windswept water, bobbing in and out amongst the whitecaps as she was swept further downstream. He prayed she wouldn't encounter a freighter or steamship in the heavily traveled waterway.

Rose was floating on her back, drifting swiftly downstream. She noticed the wide bend in the river and felt the current start to weaken. She instinctively knew that this was her chance to swim out of the current before the river narrowed and picked up speed. She turned into her breaststroke and marshaled what little energy she had, striking out vigorously towards shore. It seemed so far away, and although the current lessened, it still pulled on her. She worried she may not reach the shallows before the current resumed its speed and swept her back out. Her arms speared out and pulled the water back with wide, sweeping strokes; her legs scissor kicked out and in, like a frog, propelling her forward. In spite of her effort, she was still a long way from shore and knew she could not keep up her pace. Her arms started to feel like logs, her thinking slowed, and she felt a growing numbness all over her body. By now, she began to realize she could not swim much farther and resigned herself to her fate, her body growing limp. Her legs were sinking, unable to muster the strength for one more kick, when her toes suddenly touched sand. A bolt of adrenalin shot through her body, resuscitating her. She reached deep into her psyche, mustered three more hard kicks, stretched her hands forward, and pulled the water back vigorously with each bold sweep. She reached the shallows and stood up in waist-deep water. Exhausted and out of breath, she waded towards shore.

The taxi pulled up and skidded to a stop in the wet sand along the riverbank as Rose was climbing out of the water.

"For God's sake, Rose, what were you trying to prove? What were you thinking?" Anthony agonized, his voice filled with fear for her life, joy at her survival, and anger at her foolishness for diving into an icy, swift-flowing river. He jumped out of the cab and splashed towards her in the shallow water, a beach towel in his hand. "What if a freighter came up river? They wouldn't see you, such a small speck in the windswept river. You could have been sucked into their propellers!"

She remembered the frustrated look on his face as he stood there in the shallow water in his wet shoes and socks. *How sad he looks*, she thought, feeling sorry for him. She knew that if he could swim, he would have jumped in after her. Nevertheless, she rousted her inner strength, ignored his anger, and smiled triumphantly. "I feel so refreshed and invigorated! It was a wonderful swim. Thank you for being so understanding. I knew you would come to my rescue!" She wasn't about to tell him how close she came to drowning. He was mollified; happy she didn't drown, and wrapped the beach towel around her shivering body.

Rose remembered their enchanting honeymoon in Split, Croatia, on the Adriatic Sea, a romantic, historical place, where the azure hue of the water contrasted with the ruins of a Diocletian Palace, a place where they shared many intimate moments and planned for their future. They hiked the rocky shoreline and watched sailboats beating into the wind. They rented a room in the hillside bed and breakfast with a view of the bay below. At night, the window was kept open, allowing the sound of waves gently lapping the shoreline to lull them to sleep. In the morning, they ate freshly baked muffins and drank steaming cups of coffee in the outdoor café, watching the seagulls circling above, their white feathers contrasting against the blue sky. During the day, they frolicked in the surf. They dined on fresh seafood in cozy, nearby bistros. It was a wonderful place to return to someday when the world was at peace.

To think that none of these experiences would have been possible had she not left the security of her parent's home in Highland Park, Michigan, was almost too hard to contemplate. She knew why her parents sent her to Europe. They meant well but worried over her efforts at independence and her longing for more freedom as a teenager. It was a time of bathtub gin, home-brewed beer, speakeasies, the Lindy, and the Charleston. It was the era of Prohibition, a time when her parents decided to save her from the decadence of the roaring twenties by sending her to Europe to visit relatives and learn old world culture.

Rose, age twenty-one.

Anthony, age twenty-five.

What they did not know was that she would meet two agents from the Ziegfeld Follies on the boat to Europe and almost decided to join the dance troupe. The agents asked her to join them in Rome, their final destination, where they planned to hold auditions for several weeks. Everyone had heard of the Ziegfeld Follies, but to be approached by their representatives was a very intoxicating experience for seventeen-year-old Rose. Thoughts of stardom and glamour raced through her mind. *Yes,* she thought, *why not? How many chances like this does one get?* Deep inside, her conscience bothered her. What would her parents say and what about the relatives waiting to meet her in Trieste, Italy? Since her parents sent her to Europe, she looked at the trip as a chance to redeem herself in their eyes. But running off to join the Follies was not what they had in mind.

Noticing her hesitation, the agents said, "Rose, please take our card. It has our Rome address and telephone number on it. You are passing up the opportunity of a lifetime; call us if you change your mind." It was the last time Rose met with these two gentlemen. They stepped off the boat in Rome.

She arrived in Trieste the following evening. There was no one there to meet her. She did not have much money and, out of desperation, thought about calling the Follies agents but decided against it. How could they possibly help her from Rome? Besides, she knew her parents would be furious.

A kind-looking man in a constable uniform, standing near the pier, noticed her. She was walking off the boat with all her luggage, looking confused and frustrated. He approached her and asked, "May I be of assistance, madam? You seem to be looking for someone. Perhaps I can help."

"Thank you, but my aunt and uncle will be meeting me shortly," she remembered replying. *Where could they be?* she wondered. It was 9:00 PM. Night was approaching, and they were nowhere in sight.

"My wife and I have a spare bedroom in our apartment and would be happy to accommodate you in case your relatives were delayed somewhere," he said. "It happens quite frequently, you know. Train schedules are changed many times. Please follow me." She started to panic when he picked up her luggage and walked up the street.

She ran after him, shouting "Wait, what if they show up and I'm not here!?"

"We will call the train station from my apartment to find out when they will be arriving. Don't worry, everything will be all right. I will take good care of you," he replied over his shoulder, carrying her suitcases in each hand and quickly walking up the street.

"Put my luggage down!" she yelled. He pretended not to hear and quickened his pace. She ran after him, worried about her luggage but not knowing what else to do.

Just then, a taxi pulled up and a familiar voice called out, "Rosie, where are you going?" A big woman stepped out. With open arms, she rushed up to Rose and gave her a bear hug. It was a long time since Rose saw this formidable woman with the twinkle in her eye.

"Aunt Eva!" she cried with relief. "I almost gave up on you. It's so wonderful to see you!"

Uncle John, her mother's brother, climbed out of the taxi and asked the startled constable, "Is that my niece's luggage in your hands?"

"Why yes," he replied in a shaky voice, setting the suitcases down. "I suggested the young lady stay in my apartment tonight. The waterfront can be a dangerous place for a single woman. My wife and I have an extra bedroom."

"Extra bedroom, my foot," boomed Aunt Eva, grabbing the startled constable by the arm. "Come, I want to meet your wife!"

"No!" he yelled, surprised. In desperation, he twisted his arm out of Aunt Eva's vice-like grip and ran up the street.

"Just as I thought: another scoundrel, posing as some official, preying on single women! Come, Rosie, we are taking the taxi to the train station and the train to Kutina. Your grandparents are anxious to see you."

If it wasn't for a stern but persuasive Aunt Eva and Uncle John Schmidt she might have gotten into trouble or even become a Ziegfeld Girl. *Where does folly end and maturity begin?* she mused.

The one-hour train ride took Rose into farm country near the town of Kolin, southeast of Prague. *So much history,* she thought, gazing out the window. Nearly 150 years before, Napoleon defeated the combined armies of Prussia, Russia, and Austria near this area, at the Battle of Austerlitz. Buried shell casings and cannon balls occasionally rewarded the persistent treasure hunter, providing evidence of this bloody battle.

Rose stepped off the train into more snow. She didn't have the protection of city buildings against the blowing snow. She tightened the woolen shawl around her neck, pulled up her collar, and walked for another half-hour along the desolate road. Soon she noticed the familiar farmhouse in the distance. The well-built stone house was nearly covered with snow. Smoke was drifting out of the chimney, promising a warm hearth and a reprieve from the cold. It would have been a picturesque, serene scene if not for the war. Rose walked across the barnyard, up to the house, and knocked on the heavy wooden door. There was a long pause before it opened. A stout woman peered out with suspicious eyes.

"Mrs. Kozak!" the woman cried, recognizing Rose. "Please forgive the wait. We didn't know who it could be. These are dangerous times."

The farmer and his wife, Vaclav and Lena Verkula, welcomed Rose with open arms. "Please come and sit by the fire while I bring you some hot soup," Mrs. Verkula said. They remembered the Kozaks' from when they hiked in the area during happier times before the war, and ever since had tried to help them each time Rose came. Rose warmed herself by the fire, sipping hot potato soup.

"Mrs. Kozak, have you heard any news about the war?" Mr. Verkula asked anxiously, not having a radio. "How close are the Allies? What is happening in Prague?"

"We heard on Anthony's radio that the Allies have captured Plzen, and the Russians are in Western Slovakia, advancing towards Bratislava," Rose replied. "In Prague, the Germans are worried that the Russians will get there ahead of the Americans and send them all to gulags in Siberia. They all look for clemency from the West."

The news was well received. Mr. Verkula replied in a gruff voice, "Clemency, hell! They invaded and pillaged our country. I hope the Russians get there first and kill them all! "

Rose's trip was a success. The Verkulas needed all her sweaters. "These sweaters are just what we needed to keep our family warm," commented Mrs. Verkula. "You must let me fill your rucksack with some of our cheese, at least a couple dozen eggs, and two chickens." She asked, already bustling around, "Would you like a live duck?"

"That would be wonderful," Rose replied, before considering how to carry it. The eggs, cheese, and chickens were wrapped separately in oilpaper, but what to do with a live duck?

"We must wrap it well to hide it from the Germans," said Mrs. Verkula. "If they catch you, they will come for us. Let's take these strips of cloth," she tore several rags in half, "and wrap them tightly around her wings and webbed feet so you will be able to handle her." The strips of cloth were tightly wrapped around the duck, binding her wings and legs to her body. Her head, neck, and feet were the only visible parts sticking out of this cocoon-like package. Once her rucksack was filled and strapped to her back, she gingerly stuffed the duck into the front of her long wool coat, wrapped her gloved hands around it, and thanked the Verkulas for their generosity. Mrs. Verkula looked Rose over and asked, "It looks like a heavy load, but at least the duck is hidden inside that large coat. Are you sure you can handle it, Mrs. Kozak? Is there anything else we can give you?" "You have been more than kind," replied Rose. "I'm confident that I can manage with the duck. Thank you once again. This food will keep our family nourished for at least the next few weeks."

"Let's hope the Germans are gone by then," replied Mrs. Verkula. "Please travel safely, Mrs. Kozak. Go with God."

Rose walked out into the snow, waved one arm at the Verkulas—the other arm held the duck—and hiked back to the train stop. She knew she may have problems with the duck but was unwilling to part with such a prize. By force-feeding the duck food scraps rolled into three-inch lengths, baked in the oven until hard, she would reward her family with a two- or three-pound liver. The fat and protein would provide nourishment needed to fight the winter cold. Her problem was how to keep the duck hidden and quiet on the train ride back to Prague. Rose decided the best way to carry the duck was to keep it tucked inside the front of her heavy coat, just below her chest, with her arms around it, like cradling a baby. She allowed the duck a breathing hole between the buttons and was satisfied she could still control it with her hands.

The train was thirty minutes late. Snow was still falling. Rose waited in the desolate countryside, tired and cold. She heard the train approaching and started to wave her hands to be seen through the falling snow, but when she did this, the wily duck almost slipped out from under her coat, webbed feet flapping in the wind. Was the duck worth all this trouble? *If it wasn't for your food value, I would strangle you now and throw you in the ditch,* she thought, grabbing it by the neck and stuffing it back under her coat.

The train was crowded, but Rose found a small cramped spot by the window. A friendly man helped her take off her rucksack. She carefully pulled her arms out of the straps, one at a time, using her free arm to balance the protesting duck under her coat. She set the rucksack on the floor between her legs and eased the duck down on top of it, hidden by her large coat. The heat was suffocating and the protesting duck let out a quack, catching Rose by surprise. *I should have wrung your neck!* she thought. Luckily, the people around her were Czechs, who understood her problem. They started singing to drown out the duck's quacks. Other ducks, geese, and chickens held under similar circumstances responded with a contagious cacophony of noise, alerting the Nazi guards. As if on cue, the Czechs began singing *"Kde Domov Muy,"* their national anthem, which means "Where My Home Is." Strong arms suppressed hidden birds. Some were throttled to death by their frightened owners.

"What is this?!" exclaimed a German soldier. He stopped in front of a frightened old man, reached down, pulled his coat open, and grabbed a squawking chicken off his lap.

"Please, this is food for my grandchildren," he cried. "We are starving." Two German soldiers took him off the train at the next stop. No one knew what happened to him, but everyone suspected he would never come home.

The penalty for smuggling food was death. Rose whispered a prayer for him and thanked the Lord she was spared once again.

She returned home by late afternoon that same day, tired but satisfied that; once again, she evaded capture and accomplished her goal: bringing food home to her hungry family. She proudly displayed her bounty.

"A live duck!" exclaimed grandmother Kozak as Rose began unwrapping the wiggly bird, feet stubbornly flailing in the air. "Such a large duck, and the eggs, cheese, and chicken! How wonderful, Rose. Tonight, we feast!"

"Thank God you're safe," Anthony said, taking her in his arms. "No more trips to the countryside. It's too dangerous! The war should be over in a few weeks. We've survived so far and don't need to take any more risks."

Rose beamed with pride, happy to have contributed once again. She was filled with the excitement of the trip but most of all enjoyed her adrenalin high.

The duck was kept in a dry basement bathtub and force-fed leftover food scraps. Grandmother Kozak would hold the pesky fowl while Rose pried its beak open and stuffed the hard rolls down its throat. Rose cleaned the tub daily, covered the top with a light screen, and continued feeding the duck until it became so heavy it leaned to one side from the weight of its liver.

Two weeks later, Grandmother Julia and Rose butchered the duck, pulled the feathers off, and proudly displayed a three-pound liver. Rose made it a point to try to remember all of Julia's recipes, having watched her cook so many times over the years. Rose knew how much Anthony enjoyed his mother's cooking and was determined to cook as well. She paid attention when Julia rubbed the duck inside and out with salt and caraway seeds and noticed the cup of water she poured into a roasting pan to keep the duck moist and to prevent it from sticking to the bottom of the pan. Rose wanted to help, but Julia waved her away. This was her fiefdom and no one was allowed to interfere while she cooked. So Rose just watched as she put the duck in the oven, breast down, covered it, and roasted it for about one and a half hours, at which time she turned it over and roasted it for another hour, with the top off. This browned the skin and made it nice and crunchy. *Grandmother makes cooking look so easy*, Rose thought, wondering if she would ever be that good. When the duck was done, Julia served it with potato dumplings and sauerkraut. The liver was boiled separately in a pot. Once it was cooked, Julia allowed Rose to help by mashing the liver with duck fat, garlic, and salt. This was spread on hard-crusted rye bread and eaten with gusto. A by-product was pan-fried duck fat, called speck, cut into small cubes, salted, and eaten like candy.

Anthony surprised the family with a bottle of Hungarian red wine called Egry Bikavier, or Bull's Blood.

"How did you come by this grand possession?" asked Rose

"Don't ask. Am I not in the import/export business and is there not a black market?" Nothing else needed to be said. Everyone appreciated the risk he took.

Rose smiled knowingly. The adults each drank at least one full glass during dinner. Anthony, out of deference and love, always gave Grandfather Kozak, the family patriarch, an extra glass of wine. He was a patriotic Czech, who was critical of any occupation of his beloved homeland. Three-year-old Jaroslav sipped a half glass, diluted with water. Soon his eyes started closing, and Rose put him to bed. The Kozaks hoped for a quicker ending to the war; however, it was not to be—not yet.

As the Allies advanced towards Prague, SS and Gestapo activity increased. Hundreds of Czechs were sent to Thereisenstadt, a concentration camp north of Prague, near the Polish border.

Anthony's office, on Wenceslas Square, mysteriously burned down. Rose remembered the time she was stopped by the Gestapo and asked where Anthony's office was. She felt it had something to do with her being an American—although some friends of the family were heard to say that Anthony may have been involved with Czech partisans in some way through his work and that this was a warning. Nothing was proven. The fire was deliberately set, but all the investigations proved futile.

In 1945, as the war was ending and the Allies were approaching, there was a general uprising against the Germans, encouraged by the Russians. It was common knowledge by those who survived that the Russians, under Marshal R. Y. Malinovsky, took their time entering Prague. They let the Czechs and Germans slaughter each other so they would meet less resistance.

The U.S. Third Army, under General Patton, was forced, by treaty, to stop their advance after liberating Plzen. Each night, they heard of the fighting that raged in Prague but were unable to help.

During this time of violence, the Kozak family locked the doors, pulled heavy drapes across the windows, and stayed in the basement, using candles for light. Outside, sporadic small-arms fire could be heard as Czechs and Germans killed each other. After about a week of holding up ten miles east of Prague, the Russians finally marched into the city like conquering heroes.

Many Czechs felt betrayed. They felt Patton's army should have advanced to Prague, which would have stopped the Russians from reaching as far west as they did.

General Svoboda, who led a Czech contingent, felt ashamed. Although he was a pro-Communist, returning with the Red Army to free his homeland, the unnecessary bloodshed saddened him. The war came to an end, and soon all was forgiven and forgotten.

The speculation at that time was that if General Patton's army had been allowed to liberate Prague, the Soviet influence may have stopped with Slovakia. The Iron Curtain may have descended along the Vah River, placing Slovakia, whose population was mostly pro-Russian and agrarian, into the Communist sphere. The mostly pro-Western Czechs and Moravians would have remained free to continue their pre-war democratic government. Had this happened, Vienna and the rest of Eastern Austria may have also been spared from Soviet occupation.

Winston Churchill warned the Allies of Russian expansion into Eastern Europe. He advocated for an Allied landing in Turkey and an advance north, through what was dubbed the soft underbelly of Europe. Had this been possible, the Kozak family, and others in their situation, would have been able to resume their peaceful pre-war life, without suffering the harassment of a Communist dictatorship. However, there were too many memories of the Gallipoli tragedy during World War I, where the British, French, and Anzac (Australian and New Zealand) troops suffered severe casualties at the hands of the Ottoman Turks and the idea was dropped.

Chapter 5

Though force can protect in emergency
Only justice, fairness, consideration and
Cooperation can finally lead men to
The dawn of eternal piece

--Dwight D, Eisenhower

There was great joy and celebration for weeks to come. The Russians were heroes in Prague. Thousands of German refugees were haphazardly herded up to Masaryk Stadium, along winding Prague streets, past the square in front of the Kozak's home. It was a procession mostly of women, children, and the elderly, with all their personal belongings in their suitcases or in the rucksacks on their backs. It was a sad-looking caravan of a defeated, demoralized nation that came to conquer its weaker neighbor but now felt the same humiliation it inflicted. Many fell, exhausted, on the grassy square in front of the Kozak's home.

Rose watched this sad procession out of her front window. She didn't see them as the brutal conquerors they once were. She only saw destitute, hungry mothers, with whom she felt an affinity, trying desperately to protect their children from vengeful Czechs that were taunting them.

"The shoe is on the other foot," she said to Zdenka, who was also watching this human tragedy unfold. "I must at least try to help those poor women." She filled a pail of water, took several cups off the kitchen shelf, and walked out to help.

When she crossed the street to the grassy square, a young Czech guard grabbed her arm and asked menacingly, "Are you going to help the enemy? Have you forgotten what they did to us?"

"No, I have not forgotten what they did to us. I was raising my family during the occupation and don't need to be lectured by a young puppy like you. I am not helping the enemy. I am giving a thirsty mother and her child a drink of water," replied Rose. "If you don't wish to help me, please stay out of my way!" She walked out on to the square and gave water to the exhausted women and their children.

A young boy of eleven or twelve screamed, "They killed my mother and father. Kill them, kill them!"

"This is a mother with a thirsty child. They didn't hurt anyone," Rose replied.

The large guard approached her again and said, "You better get back in your house before someone hurts you. These people are all going back to Germany, where they belong!"

"I am an American," Rose replied calmly. "Where is the Red Cross? This situation is deplorable! These mothers and their children are starving! They need help."

The guard became more courteous but showed no sympathy toward the Germans. "They are getting what they deserve," he said. "Now please go back to your house. I will not be responsible for your safety."

Rose knew there wasn't anything else she could do and sadly walked back to her house. Angry Czechs milling around the refugees, suspicious of her motives, moved closer. Rose knew she better go into her house for her own safety and that of her family. She was not a Nazi sympathizer and certainly did not wish to appear like one.

No distinction was made between the innocent and the guilty. They had nothing to do with the war other than following their husbands. She watched with dismay as older refugees, too weak to carry their suitcases, just dropped them where they walked. Roving scavengers picked them up and ran off with them. Czech guards and their Russian counterparts just laughed and ignored them.

Rose became distressed, watching neighbors she had known for years as being kind and courteous turn into barbarians, throwing rocks, screaming, and spitting at these helpless human beings.

Dear Lord, when will this inhumanity end? she asked herself, walking into her home.

Zdenka stood in the doorway, pale and shaken, having watched the whole episode from the upstairs hall window. She was proud of her mother, and relieved by her safe return.

Weeks went by. All the Germans were gone, but now the presence of the Russian Army in Prague became a concern. Many of these so-called conquering heroes were caught looting and raping. Stories abounded of incidents of young girls and older women being accosted by gangs of drunken Russian soldiers roaming the streets at night.

A friend of the Kozaks, who lived in Slovakia died of a heart attack when Russian soldiers invaded his home, stole their jewelry—including tearing the wedding rings off his and his wife's fingers—then raped his sixty-five-year-old wife. She survived the ordeal but committed suicide shortly after. Many of these soldiers, especially the ones from the eastern provinces, were ruthless, ignorant barbarians known to stop people in the street and demand their wristwatches. People began to wonder who their real enemy was.

The Russian high command, prodded by the West, finally acknowledged the problem and instilled marshal law. A few weeks later, the Russian Army began their evacuation of Prague. The transfer of government from military to civil authority was a slow, drawn-out process. All city services were once again managed by civilians. During this transition, the trains and buses ran sporadically, and there was confusion everywhere. The mass of the Russian army was leaving but KGB agents and many Communist bureaucrats stayed behind.

Food became scarce once again. This time, it was the Russians who took everything. Rose knew it was time to visit her friends in the countryside. She packed linen bed sheets she received from her mother before the war into her large rucksack hoping to, once again, exchange them for food. She caught the 10:00 AM train for Kolin, the city that was a few miles from the Verkula farm. The train was four hours late. Rose worried she would arrive after dark. The train made many stops in small villages and finally arrived in Kolin after 10:00 PM. Military personnel of all ranks were crowding around the train station as Rose stepped off. She knew it was dangerous to walk anywhere in the dark and tried to find lodging. It proved to be a futile effort. The town was full and all the rooms were taken.

She approached an inn and pleaded with the manager, "Sir, I am by myself and am willing to pay extra for a room."

"Madam, I would like to help you. It is dangerous for a woman to be out there alone in the night, but all my rooms are filled. Why, I even have soldiers, many of whom are strangers, sharing the same rooms. Russians are leaving, Czechs who were in exile are returning, and German deserters are roaming the forests. Please be careful!" he replied.

Kolin was a melting pot of people scurrying around, looking for a safe place to spend the night. After many unsuccessful attempts to secure a room for the night, Rose decided to take a chance and walk to the farm.

She remembered hearing stories of the danger in the dark forests, so, instead of taking the shorter route through the woods, she chose to walk through the open cornfields adjacent to the woods. She cautiously picked her way through the dried corn stalks. It was the last week of October in 1945; the corn was long harvested and the remaining stalks crunched under her feet. Walking was difficult on the uneven ground. She chose her steps carefully in the partly clouded moonlight.

Rose remembered the trail through the forest, but from the cornfield, her sense of direction became confused. By circumventing the forest, she walked approximately three miles out of her way and finally reached the familiar farm by 1:00 AM, tired and thirsty. The farmhouse was completely dark. Rose stepped up to the heavy wooden door and knocked. There was no answer. After a few moments of silence, she knocked again. A small window opened above, and a frightened voice asked, "Who is there?"

"It's me, Rose Kozak, Mrs. Verkula," Rose replied. "I have walked for several hours from Kolin and almost lost my direction to your place. The bright moon helped me."

"My God, Mrs. Kozak, how did you get here at this time of night?" Mrs. Verkula asked. She opened the door in her nightgown, holding a candle in her hand, and let Rose in. "I do not want to turn on the light; it can be seen from a distance and may attract some unwelcome visitors. It is very dangerous walking in the nighttime out here! Why, just yesterday, a young girl working in the fields near the forest was raped by Russian soldiers!" She finally calmed down, closed the curtain, and set the candle on a table, saying, "Please sit on this couch. You must be tired and hungry." She gave Rose a cup of warm milk with a hunk of hard-crusted country bread and prepared a comfortable bed for her to sleep in. "We'll talk in the morning," she said and turned in for the night.

The next morning, over coffee and freshly baked rolls, they talked.

"I lost my husband of forty years to a roving band of German deserters," Mrs. Verkula said. "They came out of the woods in the early morning as my husband was milking our cow. They demanded food. He told them to leave, and they shot him in the barn. They grabbed a chicken and ran back into the woods. I think they feared the noise from the gunshot would alert a Russian patrol. I buried my husband and asked my thirty-five-year-old daughter, who lost her husband during the war, to move in with me with her two sons to help manage the farm. We must be very careful. Out here there is no law or order."

"That's such a sad story, Mrs. Verkula. I remember your husband. He was such a kind man," Rose replied. After hearing her story, she was reluctant to ask for food.

Mrs. Verkula anticipated her need and told her not to worry. "There is plenty of food on the farm; with my daughter's help, we grow our own vegetables. My grandsons milk the cows and feed the pigs. We just don't want everybody to know what we have; otherwise the soldiers would come and take it all."

The linens Rose brought were appreciated, and in exchange, Mrs. Verkula gave her a live goose. Rose was surprised and, remembering what happened during the war, said, "I had a terrible time with the duck you gave me the last time I visited. She almost got away. This goose is bigger!"

"Don't worry, Mrs. Kozak. This time we will do it right and wrap the goose up so nobody will know what you have."

The enterprising woman wrapped the goose tightly with several strips of cloth, tied her beak shut, and packed her into a box with air holes in it. They packed the goose, box and all, into Rose's large rucksack.

"I cannot thank you enough, you dear woman," Rose said to Mrs. Verkula. She gave her a hug and went on her way.

"Go with God and be careful!" she shouted after Rose.

It was broad daylight now, and Rose felt safe taking the quicker road through the woods. She passed several farmers pulling their carts to town. They were friendly and exchanged greetings in Czech. When she reached the town, she noticed a commotion near the town square.

"What is going on?" she asked a woman standing near her.

"They caught the two soldiers who raped a girl several nights before."

Her curiosity peaked, Rose walked to the square. A Russian officer asked a terrified young girl of fourteen, with tears streaming down her cheeks, "Can you identify the two soldiers who raped you?" He pointed at the squad of soldiers standing at attention.

"Yes," she cried, pointing at two very frightened young soldiers.

"You two step forward," the officer commanded. When they stepped forward, he said "Kneel!"

"Please don't shoot us," they pleaded. "We are sorry for what we did."

Deaf to their cries, he walked up behind them, pulled out his revolver, and shot them both in the back of the head, in front of their squad. Skull fragments, membranes, and blood splattered the boots of their terror-stricken comrades standing at attention.

"Let that be a lesson to all of you! We are not barbarians!" the officer shouted, putting his gun back in the holster.

Rose was aghast. She watched in horror as they dragged the dead bodies away. A stout woman wearing a babushka and a soiled apron over her dress come out of the butcher shop, filled a bucket of water from the nearby fountain, and threw it in the street, washing away the bloody debris as if nothing happened. Rose witnessed many tragic events in her life but this was one of the worst. It was corporal punishment and final. She boarded the next train to Prague, solemnly thinking about the deaths she had just witnessed. She arrived in the evening, tired and worn-out.

Her family was happy to see her return safely home. They became worried when she didn't return the night before. There were no telephones to make inquiries at that time, and Anthony thought the worst. "We thought something terrible happened to you," he exclaimed.

"The train was late. There was no way to get in touch," replied Rose, too tired to tell the whole story.

Anthony saw her worn-out body slumped in a chair and instinctively felt that something traumatic must have happened. Later that evening, Rose told him what she witnessed. "They were so young," she said.

"They were young and stupid," Anthony replied, thinking how he would feel if it happened to Zdenka. However, he felt her sorrow at having to witness such a tragedy and tried to be more understanding.

Once again, the next evening, the family celebrated with a delicious family meal. The goose was butchered, the feathers were pulled off, and a good portion of the liver that wasn't eaten was saved for later meals. It took Rose many weeks to recover from the mental anguish she felt after witnessing the execution of those two young soldiers.

The Kozak family, 1947.

Chapter 6

Keep your face to the sunshine and
you cannot see the shadows.

--Helen Keller

By 1946, Prague slowly returned to normal. In spite of a lingering Russian presence, the people seemed unaware of any approaching danger or just chose not to believe that anything bad could happen so soon after the war. On a special Sunday in late spring, Anthony woke Jaroslav up early. They ate a breakfast of soft-boiled eggs, cheese, and hard, dark bread, and drank tea. Afterwards, they walked four miles to an 11:00 AM mass at the Tyn Cathedral in downtown Prague. Anthony always dressed well for mass and made sure that Jaroslav was also well dressed. He wore a gray herringbone sport coat, charcoal pants, a white shirt, a burgundy tie, oxblood wing-tipped shoes, and a gray felt hat. Jaroslav wore herringbone knickerbockers, a white shirt, gray knee-high stockings, black shoes, and a gray woolen sport coat. They walked across the historical Charles Bridge, built in 1165, with its many statues of saints adorning each side. It extended across the Vltava River, an important waterway connecting Prague with the North Sea. Behind them, about a mile up, stood Hratchany Palace (Charles Castle), illuminated in its entire tenth-century splendor by the morning sun. It promised to be a warm day. A light breeze sent ripples across the water below, and fishermen were standing on the bank casting their lines into the river hoping to catch a pike or trout for dinner. They noticed a Russian jeep parked on the other side of the bridge, next to a restaurant. Several Russian soldiers were sitting at one of the outdoor tables, eating their breakfast. A fawning waiter hovered over them, tending to their every need.

They arrived in time for mass. The Tyn Cathedral was interesting to Anthony; it related to his love of history and his work as a forwarder. It was built in a part of Prague that became a large marketplace.

"This church was built in 1365 for foreign merchants working in nearby customhouses," he explained to Jaroslav. "Their profession was similar to mine, dealing with the transport of goods from one country to another. They needed a keen knowledge of the currency exchange to know the cost of shipping goods."

As they walked inside, Jaroslav noticed the high cathedral ceiling and the dark wooden pews, altar, and furnishings. He held on to Anthony's hand and remarked, "It looks dark and mysterious."

"But, look at the art beautifying the walls," Anthony replied. "Doesn't it brighten up the church?" Jaroslav looked up at the paintings and nodded his head to please his dad, not at all sure he agreed.

The priest said mass in Latin, which Jaroslav didn't understand but Anthony loved. He had twelve years of it in school and understood it well. He thought it gave the service a deeper meaning. He prayed that the Russians would soon depart.

Jan Huss, the Reformations priest and rector of the University of Prague in 1403, would probably have sided with Jaroslav. The Hussites were known for celebrating mass in Czech so the common people would understand it. They also allowed laymen to hold the Eucharistic Chalice. It seemed they were centuries ahead of their time. Yet, for this pious act, Jan Huss was charged with heresy at the Council of Constance in 1415 and burned at the stake.

Jaroslav felt the reverence of the mass but enjoyed the uplifting choral of Beethoven's Ninth symphony, "The Ode to Joy," more. It was an inspirational service for all those present, so soon after the war. Anthony and Jaroslav returned home in the company of all the saints standing guard along both sides of the Charles Bridge. The Russian soldiers were no longer at the restaurant. *Yes, the Germans are gone*, Anthony thought, *but the Russian presence is obvious.*

By the time they returned home, Rose and Julia had prepared a dinner of roast pork, dumplings, and sauerkraut for the whole family. Julia always sprinkled caraway seeds over the sauerkraut. For dessert, Rose baked her much-loved seven-layer mocha tort, each moist layer divided by a thick spread of mocha-flavored butter cream frosting and peach marmalade. She used one dozen eggs, one pound of butter, nuts, flour, and milk. This type of food was unavailable during the war, but now, since goods were imported from the West, it was more plentiful.

Following dinner, around 2:30 PM, the entire family walked up to Masaryk Stadium, about two miles north of the Kozaks' home, to watch the first national Sokol games since the end of the war.

The Sokols, founded in Prague in 1862, was a gymnastic organization dedicated to physical fitness and moral strength, with chapters in all Czech provinces. They were dressed in red pants and red shirts, with red pillbox hats on their heads, and came to Prague on this special day to compete for the national championship. President Benes and his Secretary of State Jan Masaryk sat in the grandstand. Next to them sat the Russian Ambassador and several other emissaries from Russia. Ice cream and hot dog vendors hawked their food. Balloons and crepe streamers floated through the air.

The Sokols high-jumped, threw javelins and the shot put, and entertained their audience with gymnastic feats until evening. The Kozak family, along with thousands of Czechs who watched the games, walked home content in their belief that all was well once again.

Movie theaters showed Western films, like *Gone with the Wind, Casablanca,* and *The African Queen,* and introduced stars like Spencer Tracy, David Niven, Lawrence Olivier, Greta Garbo, and Katherine Hepburn to the long-deprived public.

Zdenka came home from her high school one day, excitedly telling her parents, "We are allowed to read Franz Kafka once again."

Kafka was a solitary German Jew who lived and wrote in Prague (1896– 1907). One of his more popular works, *The Trial,* was widely read by students of literature and history. He wrote about people who were persecuted by the state for no apparent reason, like the way Anthony's office was burned during the German occupation or how the Gestapo routinely rounded up people without any evidence of wrongdoing.

One day, Rose decided to take young Jaroslav to see Goethe's *Faust,* playing at the Prague National Theater. She thought it would help him forget the trauma of the war and start his appreciation of the arts. It had the opposite effect. War and soldiers captivated his imagination, but something supernatural like the devil scared him. He had nightmares for two nights.

Whenever Anthony's work made it possible, they would vacation in the Krkonose Mountains near the Polish border, about ninety miles northeast of Prague. It provided a peaceful respite from the politics in Prague. Jaroslav, with the guiding hand of his mother, learned to ski there at the age of four.

Rose felt the undercurrent of political discontentment. Newspapers published stories of workers being unjustly exploited by the owners of the factories that hired them, decrying the capitalistic system. She worried that trouble may start brewing in the near future and thought it was important to keep Jaroslav physically fit in case they were forced to move quickly. She took Jaroslav skiing several times a week building his endurance and strength in his legs. He enjoyed going fast downhill but didn't know how to stop. One time, he was skiing downhill ahead of Rose, showing his mother how fast he could go. He dodged several pine trees and flew over a much-traveled road that wound up the mountain, to the lodge. Luckily, there wasn't much traffic that day. "Sit down!" Rose yelled, but it was too late. He flew all the way down to the bottom of the hill, where he finally sat down and slid to a stop. Rose caught up to him and gave him a good scolding. "How are we going to get back? We are two miles from the lodge!" They took off their skis, placed them across their shoulders, and hiked up the winding road. *This is good*, thought Rose, *at least he is building his endurance. There may come a time when he will need it.* It took them several hours to return and another hour to dry out next to a blazing hearth.

An even fonder memory of Jaroslav was when he sneaked out to go skiing by himself, only to plow into a small pine tree. He still didn't know how to stop. He hiked back with a scratched up face and a bloody nose, carrying his skis over his shoulder.

Rose was livid. "Where have you been?" she yelled. "Nobody knew where you went! Didn't you have enough the other day, skiing all the way down hill, across a main road, not knowing how to stop, putting us both in danger? You look a mess! Why didn't you tell someone where you were going? We all worried about you!"

"I just wanted to teach myself how to stop, to surprise you next time we went skiing. I tried to snow plow to a stop like you taught me, but my feet were too wide apart when I hit the tree," he sobbed, his head bent back to stem the bleeding from his nose.

Rose looked at his scratched up face. Blood was dripping out of his nose, over the front of his jacket. "What a sad-looking mess you are," she said, feeling sorry for him, her anger fading. "That was a painful way to stop," she added, amused. "We'll have to work on that snow plow; obviously you haven't quite mastered it." *At least he had the courage to try again by himself,* she thought as she stuffed pieces of toilet paper up his nose to stem the bleeding and smeared iodine on his cuts. Snowfall provided ideal skiing conditions in the winter, while the warm and pleasant summers, for the most part, provided for excellent hiking over the rugged and heavily forested terrain.

Anthony's company, Czecho-Slavia, was coming under closer scrutiny by the newly elected Communist members of government. Anthony was asked to shorten his vacations with his family and to concentrate his efforts on establishing favorable shipping terms with Scandinavian countries. As a result, the Kozaks made the most of their limited vacations.

On one such vacation in the summer, Anthony and Rose left Zdenka in charge of Jaroslav at the Pochop's Resort, where they normally stayed. Zdenka told Jaroslav to go to bed earlier than he was used to. She had plans that didn't include babysitting her little brother. After a short while, thinking he was asleep, she sneaked out to meet her boyfriend. Jaroslav was only pretending to be sleeping. As soon as she left, he climbed out the window of their second-story room, onto the roof, and into the peaceful night, to escape the darkness of his room. He lay down on the flat roof, still warm from the evening sun, and with his hands behind his head, gazing up at the stars, he slowly fell asleep with the warm summer breeze wafting over his body. When Zdenka returned later and found Jaroslav's bed empty, she panicked. *Oh my God. Where is he?* she thought. What would she tell her parents when they returned? She searched everywhere, but without success. *Where could he have gone?* she wondered in angst.

As Anthony and Rose were returning from a party at the lodge later that evening, Anthony asked Rose, "Did you listen to what the people were saying about the Communists?"

"Yes," replied Rose, "many were worried that the Communists were taking over the government and that soon they may be forced to join the Communist Party.

"What will you do if that happens?" she asked.

"I do not believe it will happen that soon. There will have to be a vote, and I don't believe that the majority of Czechs will vote for the Communists. If that happens, I'm sure we will have time to get out."

"I hope you are right," replied Rose, feeling unconvinced.

Zdenka knew she was in trouble. Jaroslav was nowhere to be found. Seeing his empty bed, Anthony asked, "Where is Jaroslav? How could you leave your little brother alone?"

"He was sleeping soundly when I left," Zdenka whined. "I was only gone for a little while." Noise from the scolding passed through the open window and woke up Jaroslav. He sheepishly climbed back in from the roof, much to everyone's relief. Zdenka scowled at him. *You little scoundrel,* she thought.

Life on Hrebenkach Street became tranquil once again. However, the Russian Embassy two blocks down the street was a busy place. Many black limousines drove in and out at all times of the day and night. The Czecho-Slavia Company rebuilt Anthony's office on Wenceslaus Square, and he resumed traveling to Scandinavian countries, looking for cheap lumber to ship back to Czechoslovakia, where it would be converted into paper and shipped to Bulgaria or Romania. Rose managed the household, tending to her children and to the needs of Anthony's aging parents. They were well into their eighties and lived in the first-floor apartment. It featured a walk out onto a brick patio, which was surrounded by a colorful flower garden which Julia, Anthony's mother, lovingly maintained.

Most Czechs enjoyed their newfound freedom. They went about their daily business, oblivious to any danger. On the political horizon, however, dark clouds were gathering. Although President Benes and Secretary of State Jan Masaryk returned from exile, Russian influence proved intimidating. Pressure for Communist representation in the Czech parliament increased. Little things, like cream cheese shipped by the American Red Cross, were clumsily repackaged with the words "Compliments of the Soviet Army" written on them. When Jaroslav took a package home from school, Rose noticed the "Philadelphia" label on the inner pack. *When will this hypocrisy end?* she wondered. Jaroslav's kindergarten was constantly subjected to war films of the heroic Russian Army fighting the Nazis. Jaroslav asked his mother, "Were the Russians the only ones fighting the Germans?"

"No!" replied Rose. "Americans, English, French, Poles, Dutch, and many others fought the Germans."

"Why don't they tell us about the Allies?" asked Jaroslav.

"Russia was also invaded by the Germans," Anthony interjected. "They suffered terrible casualties at Leningrad, Stalingrad, Moscow, and many other places. They just want us to think that they suffered the most and were our only saviors. Germany would not have been defeated without the Allied armies from the West." Jaroslav would much rather watch army movies than do school work, but he wondered if the Americans really did any fighting like his mother said.

The euphoria at the war's end was so profound that no one paid attention to such obvious warning signs. Life continued as if the Czechs were denying the possibility of any danger.

One day, while grandfather Kozak was sitting in his favorite wooden rocking chair on the patio, smoking his pipe and enjoying the afternoon sunshine, he suddenly noticed, out of the corner of his eye, a rabbit flying through the air and landing with a "thud" on the stone patio next to him. To his surprise, it began to literally rain rabbits! He looked up and saw Jaroslav hurling rabbits from the second-floor terrace, about thirty feet up.

Zdenka raised rabbits and kept them in cages along the inside wall of the terrace. Jaroslav, angry with his sister for locking him in a dark room the night before, decided to get revenge by setting her rabbits free. In his naiveté, he thought rabbits, like squirrels, could jump from heights, land on their feet, and run to freedom. So he grabbed them by their ears and flung them off the terrace with a "bon voyage," feeling like the Great Emancipator.

Grandfather Kozak shouted for Rose and Julia, "Come quick! There are rabbits flying through the air! Jaroslav is throwing them from the terrace!" Both came running and stared in disbelief at all the crippled rabbits crawling around the patio.

Hell had no greater fury than his sister when she found out what he did to her pets. "My poor rabbits," she cried. "Just wait until I get my hands on him!" Jaroslav made sure he stayed out of her way but still received punishment from his mother. "I wanted to free those poor caged-up rabbits," he wailed as she paddled his behind with a wooden spoon.

"You had no business letting the rabbits out of their cages," Rose replied. "They belonged to your sister. You did this on purpose to get even with her."

His mother and grandmother cooked hasenpfeffer (rabbit cooked with ginger snaps in a sweet-and-sour sauce) and rabbit stew for weeks to come. Fortunately, they were both excellent cooks with many tasty recipes for rabbit, one of which was roast hare with sour cream. Grandmother cleaned the rabbit, removed the membranes, and rubbed salt all over it. Rose cut the meat into smaller pieces; browned the meat in lard and bacon; fried carrots, parsnips, and celery root in butter; mixed the vegetables and meat together; and roasted it all for about one and a half hours. She then mixed sour cream and flour into the juice from the roasted rabbit, blended it together, simmered it for five minutes, and poured it over the rabbit and vegetables. Their different recipes made eating all those rabbits bearable.

Zdenka was not about to eat rabbits. "I would rather starve than eat my rabbits!" she shouted. "I'm not a cannibal!" She only ate the vegetables.

On one particularly warm Sunday afternoon, Rose, Anthony, Zdenka, and Jaroslav were picnicking with several other families in a countryside meadow about ten miles outside Prague. There were at least eight children between the ages of four and fourteen. Everyone agreed to play "capture the flag," where one-team attempts to capture a kerchief or some visible piece of cloth from the other team. Whenever a member from the opposite team is tagged while attempting to grab the flag, they become a prisoner of the home team and must help defend the flag. Jaroslav was hiding behind a bush when he saw his chance to grab the undefended flag. As he jumped up to run, he collided with Zdenka, who didn't see him and was running from a different angle, also trying to grab the flag. They landed in a heap. Zdenka jumped up first and noticed that Jaroslav was sitting in an awkward position, unable to stand. She noticed a bone splinter sticking out of his right thigh, just below his shorts. Frightened, she called for help. "Mom, Dad come quick! Jaroslav is hurt!"

Noticing her frightened look, Jaroslav looked at his thigh and started to whimper. He hadn't felt the pain because he was in shock! Hearing Zdenka's cries for help, everyone came running. Anthony and Rose wrapped Jaroslav in a raincoat and then carefully picked him up and carried him two miles to the bus stop.

Jaroslav had a broken thighbone. Technically, it was called a "compound comminuted fracture of the right femur." By the time the bus arrived, Jaroslav was losing blood and drifted in and out of consciousness. The bus driver could not leave his route to drive to a hospital, but when he neared the city limits, he stopped by a taxicab stand.

"This is as far as I can legally take you," he said. "I wish I could do more."

Anthony and Rose were grateful for his kind gesture. With Zdenka, they took Jaroslav to a hospital by taxi. Doctors set the bone and wrapped wire around the fracture to keep it in place.

Jaroslav was wrapped in a body cast that ran from his waist, down the entire length of his right leg, to his toes. It was 1946, soon after the war, so the hospital did not have access to the best medicines and sterile procedures. Within five days, Jaroslav contracted scarlet fever and was transferred to a sanitarium for contagious diseases. Doctors told Rose and Anthony that without proper antibiotics, Jaroslav didn't have much of a chance. The best they had was sulfa, a drug too weak to offer much hope.

Rose went into action. She telegraphed her sister, Josephine Ivkovich, in Reed City, Michigan, whose husband was Dr. Paul Ivkovich, a major in the U.S. Army, stationed in Berlin. Within ten days, beeswax penicillin arrived in Prague, prescribed by Dr. Paul Ivkovich, compliments of the U.S. Army. Anthony and Rose knew it was a godsend, but they also knew they had to carefully follow the trail to make sure Jaroslav received it. There was much bureaucratic jealousy in the pro-Communist sanitarium, and a wonder drug like penicillin was highly sought after.

They were able to summon the help of Dr. Hnevkovsky, a friend of the family. He was the chief of staff at Prague General Hospital, with jurisdiction over the sanitarium. Dr. Hnevkovsky considered himself a radish: red (Communist) on the outside, but white (Democratic) on the inside. His sympathies were with the West, but because of his age, his family, and his position, he would never leave Prague.

Jaroslav's nightmare grew when he started receiving shots of thick beeswax penicillin every four hours, night and day, for eight weeks. The shots were given in his left thigh or left arm. He was wide awake, screaming in terror, ten minutes before each painful shot was given. Because of the viscosity of the penicillin, the shots were administered with a long, thick needle. Rose visited every day. Anthony came with gifts whenever he was home from his business travels. He would bring toy cars from Sweden or Denmark and, with Rose, would peer and wave at Jaroslav through double-thick insulated windows, which kept visitors protected from contagious diseases. The penicillin was effective, and Jaroslav began a slow recovery.

During one early afternoon visit, Rose noticed that Jaroslav didn't respond to her presence with his usual smile. He was staring at the ceiling with a blank look on his pale face. His arms lay motionless beside his thin body, and the food next to him was left untouched.

She asked the attending nurse, "How long has he been in this condition?" The nurse, with a cigarette in her mouth, shrugged her shoulders. Seeing her lackadaisical attitude, Rose's temper flared. "I demand to see the doctor right now! I am Jaroslav's mother. My son is unresponsive to my voice. I know that something is wrong. If you are unwilling to help me, I will report you!"

The nurse felt Rose's anger. She quickly responded, in a frightened voice, "I'm sorry. I didn't realize you were his mother. The doctor in charge is in his office in another section of the sanitarium."

Rose marched the quarter mile to his office, determined to speak with him. She found the doctor sitting behind his desk, looking pale and distressed. In a soft voice, he asked what she wanted. She explained her apprehension over Jaroslav's condition. He did not feel it was his concern and suggested she speak with Jaroslav's surgeon. Rose left, annoyed at the doctor's indifference.

The receptionist caught up to her in the corridor and said, "Please forgive our doctor if he sounded unconcerned about your son. He is coping with a deep personal tragedy. His two daughters, ages sixteen and eighteen, went on a family outing last weekend. There was a lake nearby, which the sixteen-year-old decided to swim in. She swam out a short distance, inhaled water into her lungs, and started choking. The older sister swam out to help her. They struggled in the deep water and drowned. The doctor and his wife, neither of whom knew how to swim, watched in horror. He is still recovering from the shock."

"I am sorry to hear such a heartbreaking story. Please express my deepest sympathy to the doctor," replied Rose. "However, I am very concerned about the deteriorating condition of my son, and there just doesn't seem to be anyone here who can help."

"We are understaffed and under funded," replied the receptionist. "This is a state sanitarium, but suddenly our funds dried up, and the government is refusing to help. They claim that only the wealthy were allowed in the sanitarium, and that people needing special care should be able to receive it in the city hospitals. I suggest you speak with your son's doctor."

Rose, weary and sad, took the tram to Dr. Hnevkovsky's office. She arrived as he was seeing his last patient for the day.

"Something is wrong with Jaroslav," she said with concern. "I visited him today. He didn't recognize me. His eyes were glazed and he didn't touch his food."

The doctor listened with growing concern. "Mrs. Kozak, tomorrow morning, I will meet you in the sanatorium with my assistant, and we will examine Jaroslav."

The next day, they found him very weak, anemic, and listless. His eyes were glazed over and he had a fever of 102. Dr. Hnevkovsky immediately requested to have his body cast removed. They found three deep, festering sores on his back: one directly on his spine and the other two on each side of his hips. It was the direct result of poor sanitary conditions, improper patient handling, and a lack of cotton in his body cast. Dr. Hnevkovsky had his sores treated and bandaged. He noticed that his scarlet fever was no longer a problem and suggested to Rose, "Mrs. Kozak, I feel your son should be moved to a regular hospital. His scarlet fever is gone, and the hospital can provide the necessary care for his recovery."

"No!" replied Rose "It was in your hospital that Jaroslav contracted scarlet fever due to your poor sanitary conditions. I would like to treat him at home and feel I can give him better care."

"I don't blame you, Mrs. Kozak. Jaroslav will be better off away from other sick patients, provided he receives the proper care. May I recommend Dr. Neshporova to help with home visits? She is very skilled with children and specializes in contagious diseases."

Rose met with Dr. Neshporova and took an immediate liking to her. She came every day to clean the abscesses on Jaroslav's back, and gave him shots of liver extract for his anemia twice a week. Rose fed him small amounts of *shodo* every two hours, a warm mixture of raw egg yolk, red wine, and honey, beaten together. He seemed to like that the best. It was warm, sweet, and made him sleepy. She was determined to restore his health, knowing that the political situation in Prague was deteriorating. She hoped to make Jaroslav fit to travel in case the family decided to immigrate to the United States.

Day by day, he became more responsive. He started to put on weight and was smiling once again. She would take him for daily wheelchair rides in the noonday sun, and he slowly began to recover. His right leg was an inch and a half shorter than his left leg, but the doctor assured her that nature would cure that problem in time. She was focused on seeing him walk normally once again.

One evening, while Anthony was in Stockholm, Sweden, Dr. Hnevkovsky called Rose. "Mrs. Kozak, there is a new operational technique that would set Jaroslav's femur together with stainless steel screws instead of the wire that was used. I feel his leg would heal stronger and it would help him recover sooner."

"Do you really feel it will help Jaroslav walk normally again?" asked Rose.

"It is a new procedure," he replied. "They use it in the West. All their tests have proven that broken bones fuse together stronger with stainless steel screws."

"Does this mean you will have to re-break his leg?" Rose asked, concerned. "He seems to be recovering well. I would not wish to have him go through another traumatic operation unless it was very necessary."

"Mrs. Kozak," Dr. Hnevkovsky replied, "it is our hope that with the stainless steel screws Jaroslav's right leg will grow evenly with his left one. He will be under strong sedation and not feel any pain."

"I trust in your judgment, doctor, and hope it will lead to a quicker, more complete recovery."

Jaroslav was taken to the hospital. The operation was to take place by seven thirty the next morning.

However, Dr. Hnevkovsky called Rose late that night. "Mrs. Kozak I feel compelled to tell you that two young men who received these stainless steel screws today died within a few hours of their operations. The procedure was sound, but the hospital is having problems with rapidly spreading infections. Perhaps you may wish to reconsider."

Rose was troubled and didn't sleep much that night. Early the next morning, she took a taxi to the hospital.

By 6:00 AM, Jaroslav had already been prepped for the operation with a sedative. In his foggy state, he remembered his mother picking him up, out of bed, and running down the corridor with him. Nurses and orderlies ran after them. "Stop!" they yelled. "It is forbidden to do that!"

"Get out of my way!" yelled Rose. She ran out the door to the waiting cab, holding Jaroslav in her hands. She climbed into the back seat and yelled, "Drive!" to the bewildered driver. She was convinced she was saving her son's life and nobody was going to stop her.

Back home, with Rose's care and Dr. Neshporova's liver shots, Jaroslav continued to improve. Anthony would bring smoked eel, canned bananas, or canned reindeer meat from his travels to Norway or Sweden. Rose and Julia would serve these delicacies as appetizers or desserts following their staple dinner of mushroom and potato soup, dumplings, pork, and sauerkraut. One could not have eaten any better in a gourmet restaurant! Naturally, a bottle of Egry Bikavier almost always accompanied such a feast.

You would think that in Prague, Plzener Urquel beer or Budweiss from Czeske Budejovice would be found in this home. But Anthony had developed a stomach problem while traveling in Romania before the war. His doctor attributed this condition to a lack of hydrochloric stomach acid, and therefore prescribed red wine but no beer.

In August 1946, Jaroslav's grandfather, Frantisek Kozak, died peacefully on the patio, in his favorite rocking chair, newspaper on his lap, pipe still hooked in his mouth. He was ninety-one. In his prime, he was a steam locomotive engineer in Austria-Hungary, during the reign of Emperor Franz Joseph, and later, when Czechoslovakia became an independent nation under President Tomas Masaryk. He was an impassioned Czech who rejoiced the nation's independence. He threaded his train through the mountains of western Austria, through Innsbruck, Salzburg, Vienna, Bratislava, and back up to Prague. If the train broke down in the mountains, there was no one to call for help; he had to fix it with the tools he had in order to return.

Before retiring, Frantisek Kozak was the manager of the railroad turn stead in Rymarov, where locomotives were turned around on a circular platform and redirected on to other tracks. Rymarov was a city in the Northern Sudeten part of Czechoslovakia, where Anthony was born. Although Frantisek Kozak spoke German fluently, he was a patriotic Czech who was overjoyed when the Nazis were defeated and Czechoslovakia became an independent country once again. The entire family shared his love of freedom and was extremely distraught over his passing. They remembered his jubilation when President Benes was voted back into office and Jan Masaryk was made his foreign minister. With these two veteran statesmen, Frantisek felt confident that Czechoslovakia would once again be a member of a peaceful European community. He was unaware of the creeping miasma enveloping his homeland.

Chapter 7

An appeaser is one who feeds
a crocodile, hoping it will eat
him last.

--Winston Churchill

By fall 1947, Communists were elected to various ministry posts in large numbers. The circumstances seemed suspicious. Riots and bloodshed always followed these so-called elections. In February 1948, a well-organized coup overthrew the democratically elected government of Eduard Benes and Jan Masaryk, his secretary of state. All foreign nationals were asked to give up their passports, including Rose. Anthony, a Czech citizen who traveled on company business, was allowed to keep his. Cadres of KGB agents stuffed ballot boxes in all Czech and Moravian provinces. Protesters were dealt with violently. Pressure was mounting against all non-Communists at all levels of public life.

Following the Communist coup, thinking he could still make a difference, Jan Masaryk decided to stay on as secretary of state in the new government. It was a fatal miscalculation. He believed he could work with the Communists and build a bridge between the East and the West. Moscow disagreed, and he was assassinated on March 10th, 1948.

The Communists attempted to make his death look like a suicide, but all of Prague knew he was pushed out of the third-story window in the Foreign Ministry building in Hratchany Palace. President Benes abdicated, and

Prague was in turmoil. Thousands mourned as they filed past the glass casket, paying their last respect to the son of the first president of Czechoslovakia, Thomash Masaryk.

Rose, Zdenka, and Jaroslav, along with thousands of Czechs, attended the funeral ceremonies. Rose knew it was time to leave Prague. She heard that the Russians were going to replace the Czech border guards sometime that fall.

Radical left-wing action committees infiltrated labor unions and businesses alike, demanding the expulsion of all non-Communists. These were malcontents, recruited by the Communists from the bottom of the socio-economic ladder, who were promised rewards and good jobs in the new government. They bullied and intimidated anyone who was not pro-Communist. The business climate broke down, and Prague, once a prosperous city, suffered a steep economic downturn.

Businesses and industries were nationalized, and privately owned farms were placed into government-owned collectives. The farm that Rose visited when looking for food for her family during the war was placed into a collective. Friends of the Kozak family who owned businesses lost everything. The Communists called them "capitalistic parasites" and replaced the owners with government managers. Many of these alleged managers didn't know anything about the businesses they were managing. Consequently, in their egalitarian hurry to redistribute the wealth from those who built it to those who didn't, they ran large deficits, which the government was forced to reimburse through higher taxes. Life was reduced to the poverty level for everyone except government bureaucrats, the government media, and the managers of nationalized businesses.

Some demoralized business owners committed suicide, while others sought ways to escape from the country. They paid large sums of money to guides they believed to be reliable, only to find out the guides were government informers when they were caught at the border.

One evening, when the children were in bed, Rose and Anthony had a heart-to-heart talk.

"You know that it is only a matter of time before they demand you join the Party. What will you do?" she asked Anthony.

"For the time being, I feel relatively safe," he replied. "My profession is not easily learned. It requires multiple language skills and a thorough understanding of current European tariffs and the currency exchange rates in order to figure out the cost of forwarding freight and the cheapest way to insure it all. I feel that the contacts I made in the countries I visited over the years are of supreme importance. I developed them through years of mutual trust," he continued with pride. "It isn't something one learns overnight. Once the Communists ask me to start training someone, I'll start to worry."

"By then, it may be too late," Rose countered. "Why don't we make plans to immigrate to America?" she suggested. "We must be ready when the time comes to act."

"Rose, I'm forty-four years old; I don't have any contacts in America and know very little about their tariffs and international commerce. In Europe, one does not start his profession in his mid-forties. Can you imagine what it would be like for me to start all over in a foreign country like the United States?" he asked.

"All you need is your knowledge and faith in yourself to succeed in the United States," Rose persisted.

Rose wanted to push the issue but remembered her mother's words the day she left for Europe: "Marriage is not a bed of roses; you will not find happiness unless you learn to give unequivocally. Learn to forget and forgive whatever is unpleasant. Always respect the man you marry and teach your children to do likewise." Her mother was practical and wise. "Never complain," she said. "You will always have problems. We all have them, but you will have to solve them yourself. Until now, you have had our protection, but from the moment you leave our home for Europe, you will be on your own."

Remembering those words left a lump in her throat, but her mother's calm and determined attitude gave her strength. She knew that their future lay in the United States; now, if she could only convince Anthony. She could sow the seed but knew it would have to germinate into his decision.

Attempting to bolster his confidence, she said, "Your wealth of knowledge, your experience in international tariffs, and your fluency in eight languages will help you in America." She hoped he was listening, knowing well how stubborn and single-minded he could be.

"It truly is a land where opportunities abound. We could live without the fear of a repressive government persecuting people for their religious or political beliefs. Please, believe me when I say this, Anthony. Remember, I lived there for seventeen years and witnessed how well my father did. He arrived before World War I, a poor cabinet-maker who didn't speak English; but by attending night school and working six days a week, he became a craftsman in the model department at Chrysler and rose to the head of his department, providing well for his family. It would be easier for us; you have an education and speak English."

They discussed this issue frequently, and each time, the conversation ended the same: unresolved, hanging over their heads like a dark cloud.

Anthony knew he would never become a Communist and that it was just a matter of time before a decision was forced on him. Perhaps Switzerland, he mused. He knew the language and the European tariffs, and he had good business contacts there. *Would they allow me to take my family on a business-related trip?* he wondered. *It just might work,* he thought, and left it there, for now. Several days later, Anthony and Rose, along with most Czechs, were asked to bring their passports to the Ministry of Interior for safekeeping. Anthony was allowed to keep his company passport to be used for business-related travel only.

The Kozaks were friends of the American Consul Charles Tygert, a Mormon from Salt Lake City, Utah, and a neighbor on Hrebenkach. One day, shortly after Christmas 1948, while Anthony was on a business trip in Scandinavia, Mrs. Tygart invited Rose for afternoon tea. Soon after an exchange of pleasantries and small talk, Mr. Tygert came into the room and, in a somber voice, said, "Mrs. Kozak, my office received information that the new government is demanding Communist membership of all employees in all segments of businesses. I believe your husband may be in trouble upon his return. I am afraid he will be forced to join the Communist Party or be forced to resign his position."

That night, Rose made a quick decision. It was time to leave Czechoslovakia before the government could fabricate charges against Anthony and imprison him. As an American, she felt that the government would allow her family to leave. She could not contact Anthony in Scandinavia but felt she was doing what was best for their family. Several weeks earlier, she received a letter from Josephine, her sister, saying that their mother suffered a stroke. She decided to use her mother's illness as the excuse to emigrate out of the country.

Unknown to Anthony, the next day, she visited Mr. Komarek, Anthony's employer and president of Czecho-Slavia, to explain her intentions. "Mr. Komarek, I have a favor to ask you. We have known each other's families for many years. You know that I am an American. I received news that my mother is very ill. I have not seen her in over eighteen years and wish to immigrate to the United States with my family, to see her once again before she dies."

"Does Anthony know anything about this?" asked the surprised man.

"Not yet," replied Rose, "but I am confident that he will wish to leave. We have discussed this possibility several times in the past few months, and Anthony agreed that his future would be better served in the West."

"Perhaps we can make some arrangement to have you and your children visit with your mother for a short time. Anthony will stay here to continue his work. Now that we have a new government, we must keep our relationships with our trading partners in the West strong so we can rebuild our economy.

Anthony has many excellent resources there that will help us. We have been friends for a long time, and he is a valuable director in our company. I know that once I convince him of the benign nature of this government, he will have a wonderful future with us. How does that sound to you, Mrs. Kozak?"

"Anthony worries about the direction the new government is taking."

"In other words, he does not wish to join the Communist Party?" asked Mr. Komarek suspiciously.

"No, he does not," replied Rose, completely unaware of the danger she created for Anthony and her family. She felt that since Mr. Komarek was a trusted friend and Anthony's business associate, he would understand her request and help them. There was no way Rose could telephone Anthony in Finland to consult with him first. She felt that she needed to take immediate action to get her family out of the country and hopefully stop Anthony from returning.

She didn't know that, by now, Czecho-Slavia was nationalized and Mr. Komarek had become a Communist. She didn't realize the political consequences of her request and the sudden danger to Anthony, who had not yet proclaimed his allegiance to the Communist Party. She knew he would be required to do so shortly, if he wished to stay with Czecho-Slavia, but did not believe it would happen this soon.

Rose sent a message to Anthony, through the American Consul's office, explaining what she had done, hoping he would approve. She thought it was a safe way for them to leave a deteriorating situation.

Several days later, Mr. Tygart visited Rose to tell her he heard the Communists planned to seize Anthony upon his return.

"Mrs. Kozak, we intercepted a memorandum to the effect that your family wished to immigrate to the United States and that by now your husband should have joined the Communist Party. Your husband is on their list of people to detain and question. I think you know what that means."

Rose suddenly realized the folly of her deed. "My Lord," she cried, "what have I done?" It seemed that not so long ago, Miro Komarek, Karl Svetensko (another director of Czecho-Slavia), and Anthony were the best of friends. Their families hiked together, picnicked together, and talked about wonderful business opportunities for the company after the defeat of the Nazis and the rebirth of Democracy under Dr. Benes and Jan Masaryk. They all believed in the capitalistic system of free enterprise, the way it was before the war. This post-war period seemed to be a good time for new beginnings and new hope in the future, with opportunities for all. Anthony, the Komareks, and the Svetenskos hoped to spin off their own forwarding company, perhaps as a subsidiary of Czecho-Slavia, and relocate near the city of Chep, in the

Sudetenland close to the German border, an area considered favorable to their future business.

All these dreams, Rose soon realized, came to an end with the Russian subjugation of Czechoslovakia and the advent of Communism. She didn't comprehend that it would happen so soon or the consequences it held for the directors of Czecho-Slavia. She was still under the impression that there was going to be a vote as to which of the directors wished to join the Communist Party. She soon realized that there was no vote and that in the unlikely event the directors did not join the Communist Party they would lose their jobs. In spite of any promises by the government, Czecho-Slavia was nationalized. The directors worked at the whim of government overseers.

How naive of me, she thought. *I should have seen this coming.* She worried about Anthony and the danger she put him in. Not being the type to dwell in misfortune, Rose quickly sent a message, with Mr. Tygart's help, asking him not to return but to seek political asylum in the West.

"My dearest Anthony," she wrote, "please forgive me. I didn't realize what they would do to you. I only did what I thought was best for our family. Please do not come back; they are waiting to imprison you. I am an American citizen so they will have to allow me and our children to leave."

She still felt that as an American citizen, she and their children were protected by international laws allowing her to return to the United States. At the suggestion of Mr. Tygart, she made an appointment to see his friend Mr. Slepak at the Ministry of Interior (homeland security), who she was told may be sympathetic to her request. Mr. Slepak welcomed Rose into his office. "How may I be of service to you, Mrs. Kozak?" he asked congenially.

"I would like to immigrate to the United States with my children," Rose replied. "I just received news that my mother suffered a stroke. I have not seen her in eighteen years and would like to see her once more before she dies."

"I am sympathetic to your situation," replied Mr. Slepak, "but I represent state security, not the Department of Emigration, where you must go. They will decide on your emigration request, not I. Should you require safe passage sometime in the future, I may be able to help. Please stay in touch."

Preposterous! thought Rose. She knew the Ministry of Interior had the power to intervene wherever and whenever it suited them. Nevertheless, she thanked him, knowing that she may need his help sometime in the near future.

She went to the Ministry of Emigration with her wish to emigrate to the United States. She met with Mr. Jan Havlechek, who listened to her request. "Mrs. Kozak," he replied, "you are free to leave, but your children must stay. Jaroslav and Zdenka were born in Czechoslovakia; they are Czech citizens, not Americans, like you. As soon as your husband returns, you are free to go."

"My children are Americans through my blood," Rose replied hotly. "That is a well-known international law. Why can the Czech government not abide by this law? Do you not honor the international law of *jus sanguis* or *jus soli* (citizenship through blood of parent or country of birth)?" According to international law, Jaroslav and Zdenka would have had dual citizenship.

"Our new government is not beholden to other countries' laws," Mr. Havlechek replied testily. "When your husband returns, we will look more favorably at your request to immigrate to the United States."

So that's it, thought Rose. *They want Anthony and are holding us hostage until he returns, at which time they will arrest him and allow me and my children to emigrate out of Czechoslovakia. No, I will not allow that to happen. Not without Anthony. There must be another way.*

She smiled at Mr. Havlechek and said, "Thank you for your time. I'm sure Anthony will return soon, and we will both visit with you in the near future."

Anthony received Rose's letter in Helsinki, Finland, and read it in disbelief. He knew from her first message that he was finished at Czecho-Slavia. He could never be a Communist and knew that his chances of supporting his family in the fashion they were accustomed to in Czechoslovakia were gone.

When he received her second message, he knew he would be imprisoned if he returned. At first, he was very angry with Rose. *What could have possibly possessed her to commit such a foolish act?* he wondered. Deep inside, his pride hurt. He was the head of the family, the chief provider, and the chief decision-maker, all of which he felt was now usurped from him. Yet, at the same time, he knew he procrastinated on his decision to not join the Communist Party. Rose's action forced the decision on him. He just didn't expect events to happen so quickly. It was time to act on his convictions. Was he brave enough? He wondered. The safety of his family meant everything to him.

How would he live without his family if he were unable to return? He knew that the political turmoil and bureaucratic confusion in Czechoslovakia might compound Rose's efforts to immigrate to the West, but he was unaware of Rose's inability to leave the country with their children. He had a fourteen-day visa, after which time he was required to return. His mind was in turmoil.

Feeling that Rose was safe as an American citizen, he telegraphed his friend and business associate, Mr. Rittman, publisher of *Transport Magazine* in Basel, Switzerland, and explained his dilemma. Mr. Rittman knew Anthony well, having visited with him on many business occasions in Bratislava and Prague. He considered Anthony's knowledge a valuable asset to *Transport Magazine* and offered him a position as a translator and writer. Anthony was overjoyed but knew he needed a transit visa to enter Switzerland and that it may only be obtained through the Swiss government.

The Swiss had a very protective immigration policy. However, with Anthony's promise to eventually immigrate to the United States, and with Mr. Rittman's insistence that Anthony's work was needed at *Transport Magazine,* they allowed Anthony to enter Switzerland on a temporary work-related visa.

Anthony was troubled at having to leave his family behind. Instead of traveling directly to Switzerland, knowing he had eleven days left on his visa, he decided on a secret trip back to Prague. He needed to validate his family's emigration plans with Rose and to reconcile his troubled feelings towards her before his final departure to Basel. *Do we still have a future together?* he wondered

With all the problems the government was having converting to a Communist system, Anthony didn't feel they would pay much attention to him. He still had a valid company passport and eleven days on his visa. He needed to have a serious discussion with Rose, to clear the air. What was she thinking? He was fuming with frustration. He knew he would never become a Communist but felt there may have been a more prudent way to leave the country—perhaps a business trip, which may have allowed his family to travel with him. Did his wife feel he was not up to the task? His European ego troubled him. Whatever happened to the Latin term *Mos Maiorum,* the established order of things? His mother never questioned any of his father's decisions; after all, the man was the head of his family. Were all American women such individualists, so impulsive? He could only theorize what her motives may have been but was resolute to find out.

Chapter 8

*You don't tell deliberate
lies, but sometimes you have
to be evasive.*

--Margaret Thatcher, speaking on diplomacy

At five o'clock the next morning, Anthony boarded a train that took him from Helsinki, Finland, into Russia. He knew the trip to Prague would take at least two days, perhaps longer. The train crossed a strip of land between the Gulf of Finland and Lake Ladoga. Once across the Russian border, near the city of Vyborg, the passengers were transferred into a sealed car manned by Russian troops. Because the train traveled near a secured Russian arms depot and mobilization center, the windows had sheet metal bolted over them, preventing anyone from observing military maneuvers. Noise from heavy machinery and marching troops could be heard outside. No one was permitted to leave their seat during this challenging train ride. Armed Russian soldiers stood guard in each car. They rode in silence; No one spoke a word.

Once the train cleared the secured area, somewhere near the city of Leningrad, the passengers were transferred to a regular railroad car with windows. Evidence of the war was everywhere. Bombed-out buildings, uprooted trees, and deep craters were visible testimonials of the destruction suffered by the Russians at the hands of the German war machine. The countryside outside Anthony's window was desolate: no roads, people, or animals, just miles of snow-covered fir trees and frozen lakes.

The date was February 1949. Anthony continued his lengthy train ride from Russia; through the Baltic states of Estonia, Latvia, Lithuania; down across the flat farmlands of Poland; over the Sudeten highlands; into Czechoslovakia and finally Prague. He arrived at 11 PM, two days after starting his journey, surprising Rose and Zdenka.

Rose was changing into her nightgown, getting ready for bed, Jaroslav was sleeping, and Zdenka was finishing her homework, when she heard the lock on the front door click. The door opened to the length of the short safety chain. Alarmed, Rose threw on her robe, grabbed a steel poker from the fireplace, and demanded, "Who is there?" ready to strike the hand that would reach for the inside lock. Zdenka picked up a steel frying pan off the stove and stood behind her mother.

"Anthony," cried the tired voice. He didn't wish to ring the door bell for fear of waking everyone.

Anthony's return to Prague from Helsinki, Finland.

Jaroslav was asleep in the next room. He woke up to Rose and Zdenka's cries of joy. He ran into the kitchen, where they all congregated, and threw his arms around his dad's neck. The family enjoyed a short but happy reunion.

"How in the world did you get here?" asked Rose surprised. "I thought you would be in Basel, Switzerland, by now. Why did you come? If the Ministry of Interior finds out you are here, you will be arrested. They have informants everywhere!"

"Don't worry; I still have nine days left on my visa. They are too busy with their new government to be looking for me, but I don't have much time." Anthony looked into her eyes, clasped her hands, and quietly said, "We need to talk.

"What possessed you to approach Komarek and tell him we wished to immigrate to the United States without discussing this with me first? Didn't you know or even suspect that he was a Communist by now? You placed our family in jeopardy!"

Rose broke down and cried. "No, I didn't think he was a Communist. He was always such a good friend of ours. You two were discussing the possibilities of starting your own forwarding business after the war. Communists don't talk like that. What happened to him?"

"He was trying to survive, to save his family. He would have turned me in to save his job. Czecho-Slavia is nationalized. They are all Communists," Anthony surmised sadly. "Be careful of Svetensko if he comes looking for me. He was always talking about the fairness of a Communist system."

"I'm so sorry, Anthony; I only wanted to help. I thought that because I am an American, they would let us all go. I told them my mother was sick and that I have not seen her in eighteen years, hoping they would show leniency. I'm sure they will allow me and the kids to go," she lied.

Anthony and Rose had their discussion, at the end of which, they consoled each other. He loved her in spite of what happened and knew that what she did came from the heart; he forgave her.

They decided that he must escape to Switzerland, where he would be safe. Rose wanted to convince him that as an American citizen she would be allowed to emigrate with her children after him. She didn't dare tell him that the Communists denied their children the right to emigrate for fear he would stay and be captured. Her stomach was tied in knots. What else could she do? she thought, feeling sick that she deceived him.

Anthony seemed to read her thoughts. "Rose," he asked, "what if they do not allow you and the kids to emigrate and decide to hold you hostage forcing me to return?" Rose was aghast that he should even suggest such a possibility. It was exactly what she feared.

"What do you propose?" she asked, unsettled.

"Suppose we fabricate a divorce?" Anthony suggested. "If we make it believable, the Communists could no longer hold you hostage. When I reach Switzerland, you wait a few weeks and then cry to all our friends that I left you to make it sound believable. Next you go to the government, claim abandonment, and file for divorce. When the divorce is granted, they could no longer deny you the right to immigrate to the United States to visit your ailing mother. We would unite in Switzerland, remarry, and continue our life as a family."

"Boy, you seem to have it all figured out!" Rose replied, emotionally. "How long have you been planning this? It seemed to come out with such ease."

"Don't talk foolishly. You think that I would travel from Finland to Prague, risking imprisonment, if I wanted a divorce?" he asked harshly. "I could have just as easily stayed there. My suggestion would guarantee you and our children safe conduct to the West where we would reunite. But you must make it believable." Rose felt hurt but reluctantly agreed.

Early the next morning, at the Prague national train station, she kissed him good-bye, not knowing if she would ever see him again. Anthony boarded the train to Switzerland, despondent from leaving his family once again. Tears welled up in his eyes as he watched his family waving good-bye to him from the station platform. The train slowly gathered speed and pulled away. He consoled himself with the thought that the family would soon reunite in the West. It was the only way out.

On the train, he shared a compartment with Dr. Benjamin Feldman, a Zionist Jew, who was expelled from Prague for attempting to recruit Czech Jews to immigrate to Palestine, where a new state called Israel was being created. All seemed well until the near empty train stopped at the Czech-German border. The few people on board were herded into a customs house, where they were strip-searched by armed border guards. Anthony's visa and passport came under suspicious scrutiny. His visa did not have the newly required date of departure stamp on it.

The young border guard who studied Anthony's visa looked up and said, "I am sorry, Mr. Kozak, but you will have to return to Prague and have your visa corrected. I cannot allow you to pass into Germany."

"That is preposterous!" Anthony replied. He knew he would be imprisoned if he returned. "Take me to the officer in charge!" he demanded.

The young border guard felt Anthony's anger and sought out the chief customs official. A portly man in an ill-fitting, rumpled, blue uniform, with a silver badge on his chest approached Anthony. He haughtily asked, "What is your problem? I am very busy."

"Your guard will not allow me to travel to Switzerland without some newly required date of departure stamp. I have traveled from Finland to Prague in the past several days and received a new directive from my company to travel to Basel, Switzerland, as soon as possible. I have an in-transit visa and do not require a date of departure stamp. I am traveling on Consular business," Anthony told him. "If I am not allowed to travel to Switzerland, you will be held responsible for impeding the free flow of trade. Mr. Slepak at the Ministry of Interior will hear about you!"

Rose told him about Mr. Slepak, and he thought it would be a good time to use his name. Anthony's authoritative tone mollified the peasant guard. He feared any government involvement.

"I will allow you to cross the border on the condition that you promise to stop in Munich and call customs officials in Prague to correct your visa stamp problem and exonerate me from any wrongdoings."

"I promise," Anthony told him, knowing that the less said the better. At this time, nobody in government knew he was on the train. If he made the call, he would alert the authorities and place his family in danger, and the custom official would lose his job for allowing him to escape.

Back on the train, Dr. Feldman asked, "Mr. Kozak, are you really going to get off this train in Munich to make that call? I strongly suggest against it."

Anthony, much relieved to be on the train and attempting to relax himself, replied, "Dear doctor, thank you for your concern, but I am not leaving this train until it stops in Basel, Switzerland. A team of wild horses could not pull me off!"

Chapter 9

*Never mention the worst. Never think
of it. Drop it out of your consciousness.*

--Norman Vincent Peale

Once in Switzerland, Anthony explained his dilemma to the Swiss government. They were understanding and allowed him to stay until his family joined him, at which time they would immigrate to the United States. Then the sad news struck. Anthony received news from the Czech consul in Basel that the Czech government would not allow Rose to leave with their children. He quickly sent a telegram to Rose at Mr. Tygart's office in Prague, through the American consul in Basel:

> *My anxiety is growing over leaving you and the children. I'm tortured
> with guilt having left you behind. There are no words to express how
> much I miss you all. Please follow the program we decided on the night
> before my departure. I pray for your safe trip out and our reunification.
> Love, Anthony.*

He then sent letters to the American Embassy in Bern, suggesting that the American Embassy in Prague offer his family protection. He wrote Rose's parents, James and Hedwig Kousak, and Rose's sister and brother-in-law, Josephine and Paul Ivkovich, in Reed City, Michigan, beseeching them to help through political connections or any other possible way. Letters and telegrams flew back and forth. Josephine and Paul tried their best by asking Michigan Senator Arthur Vandenberg's office to intervene on Rose's behalf.

67

In the meantime, the Czech Ministry of Interior learned of Anthony's escape to Switzerland and sent an urgent request to the Swiss government that he must return or face prison and the loss of all his possessions and property. Anthony knew that the loss of possessions may happen but did not expect any criminal charges. How low would they go? he wondered, afraid for his family.

The Czech Communists fabricated criminal charges against Anthony and demanded that the Swiss send him back. Mr. Rittman at Transport LTD, who had known Anthony for many years, convinced the Swiss of his value to Transport LTD. The Swiss responded by offering Rose and her children a transit visa to Switzerland.

The Czechs said no.

Rose was at her wit's end. The Czech Ministry of Interior informed her that they had knowledge of Anthony's defection to Switzerland. They told her that criminal charges would be made against him and that if he didn't return by the time his visa expired, all of their possessions and property would be taken away.

Rose thought about fabricating the divorce they discussed but decided against it. She felt it would be too emotionally difficult on the children. To make it look real, she would need to convince them that their father actually did abandon them. She would be unable to tell them that it was merely a ruse to fool the Communists, for fear of exposure. She knew how kids always talked and enjoyed telling each other secrets. It would not take long for a teacher or parent to overhear remarks that would expose her. It would be equally troublesome for her to fool her relatives and friends. Those who knew Anthony well would not believe that he would abandon his family. This would result in questions she would be hard-pressed to answer. Instead, Rose decided to tell everyone that Anthony was on another business trip and that he would return soon. She would also tell the Communists that Anthony felt remorse and would return to face his charges.

Antony Kozak   Basle, February 26th 1949.
Basel, Spalentorweg 9.

                    To
                    The American Consulat General,
                    Bahnhofstrasse 3
                    Z ü r i c h .
                    ═══════════════

Re: Immigration.

                I refer to my last visit on 23rd inst, during
which I tried to describe you our situation, especially my family's
situation in Prague and beg to inform you, that I received a letter
to-day from my wife, asking me, you may summon her trough the American Embassy in Prague, to come to Zürich for registration.
                May I be allowed to repeat briefly our situation:
Last autumn, when we applied for immigration, I was told, it will be
nearly impossible to immigrate owing to the small quota for Czechoslovakia and that the sole possibility is, to go abroad legaly and to
wait there, the family would be allowed to follow, since family members
are not separated. Therefore a gave notice to my firm and be~~came in~~
possession of a ~~passport~~, valid till December 31-1948, I came to
Switzerland on December 17th 1948 during my legal leave. The Swiss
authorities granted me the possibility to work at Messrs. Rittmann &
Bauer A.G., editors of "Transport", Basle, to whom I was correspondent
for Czechoslovakia since 1945.
                After my passport expired, I applied for the im-
migration passport through our legation but was refused last week and
summoned to return, otherwise I shall be punished by 1-5 years of jail.
To make the situation more grave, a legal proceeding was opened against
me for a pretended damage I caused my former firm. Needless to say,
that it is a lie, only to prevent our immigration by all means.
                I beg to point out, that my wife is the child of
American citizens and that she was since her 3rd month of age till 1930
in the U.S.A.
                Please do us the favour in the above mentioned way
and excuse me, having bothered you once more.

                                        Yours respectfully

registered.

P.S. The Swiss visa was granted
on 21 inst. telegraphically.

Anthony explaining his circumstances to the American Consul,
February 26, 1949.

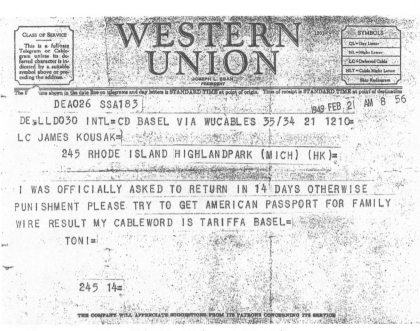

Telegram, February 21, 1949.

Rose pretended to be surprised at the government's charges, but knew there would be repercussions for Anthony's refusal to join the Party. That's why she asked him not to return. She decided to call on Mr. Slepak at the Ministry of Interior and was granted an appointment the following day. The next day, as she approached the stately building near Hratchany Palace, she noticed two flags visibly flapping in the wind on top of the balustrade: one was the red, white, and blue Czech flag; the other was the Russian red flag with a yellow hammer and sickle in the upper left corner. She walked past two armed guards standing at attention on each side of the entrance and opened a heavy metal door, which led into a cathedral foyer. She gave her identification papers to the grim, white-haired lady in a gray suit sitting at the only desk in the middle of this hall. There were no chairs to sit on. *It looks so stark*, thought Rose. After she had stood there for fifteen minutes the telephone on the desk rang. The lady answered it, stood up and, in a clipped voice, said, "Mr. Slepak will see you now. Come with me." She led Rose down a stone corridor, their footsteps echoing across the hallway, to a wooden door. There was a guard standing at attention next to it. She knocked on the door and opened it into a thickly carpeted, lavish office. Mr. Slepak, a slender, well-dressed man in his mid-fifties, wearing a blue tailored suit, a white shirt, and burgundy tie, stood up from behind his polished mahogany desk. He set his lit cigarette in an ashtray, walked up to Rose with a smile, shook her hand, and, in a friendly voice, asked, "To what do I owe this pleasure, Mrs. Kozak?"

"Mr. Slepak, Anthony misses his family and will be coming home soon to prove his innocence. I worry for his safety and would like your assurance that nothing will happen to him."

"It gives me great comfort to know that your husband is returning to face his charges." As an afterthought, he asked. "Will he be joining the Communist Party?"

"Why, yes," Rose quickly answered, wondering if he was trying to trap her. "He decided that it would benefit his career and the well-being of our family."

"In that case," Slepak answered, "I will do all I can to exonerate him of those charges."

"Thank you for your help," replied Rose, much relieved. She noticed the pack of Chesterfields sitting on his desk. *What a hypocrite*, she thought, *espousing the virtues of Communism while smoking American cigarettes.* They shook hands and she quickly walked out of his office. Yet something bothered her. It went too smoothly. She turned her head and saw Slepak standing in the doorway, smiling, holding a lit cigarette in his hand. *Did he really believe me?* She wondered, noticing that his steel blue eyes did not reflect the warmth in his smile. She quickly walked out of the austere building, hoping the meeting bought her time to plan.

Grandmother Julia, feeling the loss of her husband, grew increasingly weaker. After several months, she suffered a stroke and died in March of 1949. Rose knew how close Anthony was to his mother. When Julia's sister was dying of tuberculosis, she made Julia promise to marry her husband, Frantisek Kozak, and raise their children, Olga and Zdenek. Several weeks following her sister's death, Julia Niemez married Frantisek Kozak. Anthony was their only child.

With a heavy heart, Rose wrote the following letter to Anthony:

> *Dearest Anthony,*
>
> *It is very difficult for me to write this letter. Your mother passed away yesterday afternoon, March. 26, 1949. Anthony, I feel so sorry for you. I know the sadness you must be feeling at this moment, being all alone. Please bear in mind that it was the Lord's wish to relieve her pain from a debilitating stroke. Be thankful she found peace. We are all grieving with you and were at her side when she passed away. I look for the day when we are once again united as a family.*
>
> *With all my love,*
>
> *Rose*

The day before Julia's funeral, Rose visited the mausoleum where Frantisek's ashes were interned. She removed his urn from the glass shelf where it was displayed, took it to the funeral home, and, with Zdenka's help, placed it into Julia's coffin without anyone's knowledge. She felt better that Julia and Frantisek were together and knew that Anthony would have approved.

The next morning, following a funeral mass for Julia, Rose, Zdenka, Jaroslav, and their relatives and friends, walked one mile to the cemetery, behind a horse-drawn hearse. It was a dreary, overcast Saturday morning. The hearse was made of wood, with four large, wooden, spoked wheels. Large glass panels on each side were etched with flower designs around the edges, outlining Julia's coffin inside. It was drawn by a large black horse with a black flower tassel attached to the top of his head. The driver looked solemn, dressed in black, with a large top hat on his head.

Afterwards, a few relatives and friends came to the Kozak home, where they ate cookies, drank coffee, and lamented Julia's passing. Others stayed away, knowing of Anthony's refusal to join the Communist Party and his escape to Switzerland. Some, who did not know the circumstances, thought he left his family to save himself. They did not wish to be implicated in any way. It was a grim day.

Rose noticed that a neighbor friend of theirs, Mrs. Milakova, was avoiding her and others in the neighborhood. She was the wife of a well-known textile merchant, whose firm had been nationalized in recent months.

The following evening, she saw Rose in front of her house and approached her cautiously. She gripped Rose's hand tightly and whispered, "I heard they refused to let you immigrate to Switzerland. Be careful! My husband and I had decided to leave the country with our three daughters. We contacted a person who we believed would help us, only to be caught at the border by the secret police. I have no idea what happened to my husband. They took our house away but allowed me to stay in two rooms with my daughters. The rest of the house was divided amongst several civil servant families. Listen to me: don't trust anyone, not even your closest friends. We are constantly watched wherever we go. Be careful!" Rose was shaken. She had not seen this woman in weeks but had heard that the family was in trouble with the government.

"Thank you for your concern," Rose answered guardedly. "I don't know what you have heard, but my husband is returning soon and we are not leaving Prague."

Mrs. Milakova gave Rose a knowing smile, released her hand, and said, "Good for you. You are learning."

Rose returned home and told Zdenka what had just happened. "Please be careful what you say to your friends in school. How would Mrs. Milakova know we wanted to immigrate to Switzerland? We must be careful of what we say, even to good friends." Rose worried she gave out too much information.

Many people were sent to Siberia, never to be heard from again. Any dissidence was crushed. It was a prelude to Stalin's grand design for the subjugation of Eastern Europe.

In April of 1949, Rose decided to make a pilgrimage to Bila Hora (White Mountain), a shrine built on the grounds where Catholic Hapsburgs defeated the Reformationist Hussites in November of 1620. She had a deep faith in God and believed in the power of prayer. *How many times did the hand of Divine Providence guide me to safety?* she thought. Her prayers for guidance and for Anthony's forgiveness gave her a feeling of peace. In the gift shop she purchased a framed etching of Michael the Archangel guiding two lost children near a deep stream. She wrote the date on the back: April 6, 1949. Feeling spiritually refreshed, she returned to Prague and began formulating a plan.

She started by writing a letter to her sister, Josephine, and her husband, Dr. Paul Ivkovich, in Reed City, Michigan, explaining her dire state of affairs and hoped that through their friendship with elected officials, pressure could be directed at the Czech government. She didn't know that Anthony was also frantically writing letters to them and her parents, as well as to the Swiss and American Consulates, trying desperately to bring his family to Switzerland.

Rose was at a loss as to why the American Embassy in Prague refused to help her. Each time she visited the embassy, she was asked to wait, sometimes for hours before being told that the person she was to see had other, more pressing, commitments or that the person was replaced by someone else. She sought an appointment with the American ambassador, Laurence Steinhardt, but was given the run-around and wondered why. She knew there was political turmoil in Prague but could not understand why the American Embassy refused to help an American in distress. Later that week, she was told that Ambassador Steinhardt was being transferred to Canada and that his position became untenable. She knew it was useless to go to the Czech government and ask for her passport. They denied ever having it and asked why she would need it since she wasn't traveling out of the country.

Chapter 10

If a nation expects to be ignorant
and free in a state of civilization, it
expects what never was and never will be.

--Thomas Jefferson

For many years Rose thought she was born in Dayton, Ohio and considered herself to be an American. She was the oldest of six children, born on August 7th, 1907. Three girls and three boys were born to James and Hedwig Kousak. Rose's brother Jim was two years younger and Josephine, her sister, was five years younger, followed by Sonny, Ann and Charlie. Her father, James, was a Czech born in Stare Boleslav, a city in the Czech portion of Austria-Hungary, while her mother, Hedwig Schmidt, was one of twelve children born to a German brick manufacturer in Glatz, Silesia. James and Hedwig met in Kutina, a city in the Croatian part of Austria-Hungary, which later became a part of Northern Yugoslavia and today is independent Croatia.

Rose felt despondent and alone. She remembered living in Dayton, Ohio, from a very young age and felt that if she could only get her passport back from the Czech government, she could prove her nationality. She remembered her mother's story of how she met her father and the problems they overcame in their effort to reach the United States. She realized how closely her problems were related to those of her parents.

Rose remembered the story her mother told her years before, how the Hapsburg government enticed business people and skilled craftsmen with cheap land and low taxes to settle in the Croatian part of their empire. The Schmidt family moved to Kutina, seeking a favorable business environment. They purchased several acres of land and continued with their brick manufacturing business. James Kousak was in Kutina finishing the sixth and final year of his fine cabinetmaker apprenticeship.

Hedwig was betrothed to an Austrian cavalry officer at that time, but when she found out that he had a mistress in Vienna, she broke the engagement. She met James while shopping for furniture at a cabinetmakers shop with her mother. Her mother noticed the beautiful handcrafted furniture and asked the owner to build a cabinet for her china. Hedwig noticed James, who was working in the shop. She was drawn to his wide smile, kind eyes, rugged composure, and strong hands. The owner asked James, "How soon can you build a cabinet for the lady?"

James thought for a minute, smiled at Hedwig, and replied, very self-assured, "In two weeks the lady will have the finest cabinet in the empire. Why, Franz Joseph himself could not have a better one built."

Hedwig created all sorts of reasons to visit his shop and check on the cabinet. They fell in love, against her parent's wishes.

"He is not good enough for you," warned her family. "What kind of future will you have with him? You are German; he is Bohemian. Your sisters and brothers all married Germans."

James was proud to be a master cabinetmaker and knew he would be able to support Hedwig should they be allowed to marry. He said to the Schmidts, "I love her and will provide well for her if she will have me."

Hedwig was extremely stubborn and persuasive with her parents. They finally relented and, although reluctantly at first, accepted James into their family. James and Hedwig were married in a Roman Catholic Church by Hedwig's uncle on her mother's side, Johan Nestler, one of three brothers who became missionary priests. He traveled down from Silesia to perform the wedding ceremony. Later, all three Nestler priests traveled to Africa to spread the gospel but were never heard from again.

Kutina was a peaceful place with economic opportunities and plenty of work for all. The Schmidts' brick manufacturing went well, and James Kousak became known as the most skilled cabinetmaker in town.

Life seemed good; however, further south and east, trouble was brewing. The Eastern Orthodox Serbs (Slavs) wanted their independence from the Muslim Ottoman Turks occupying their land and looked forward to establishing their hegemony over the other Slavic territories in the Hapsburg Empire to their north and west. They wished to reestablish their old Kingdom of Serbia the way it was, before Ottoman Turkey invaded their land.

With political trouble spreading north, James and Hedwig decided to immigrate to the United States. Hedwig's mother did not want her daughter to leave and tried her best to persuade them to stay.

"How will you get along in a strange country? You don't know the language! You don't have any job prospects! Just how do you expect to support my daughter?" she asked, looking accusingly at James.

"In America, there is a future for cabinetmakers like me," replied James. "People from all over the world are immigrating to America; they are building homes and will need furniture. We do not wish to raise a family in this politically unstable empire."

Hedwig's mother, realizing she could not change James and Hedwig's minds, suggested, "Since you have decided to go, at least move to Dayton, Ohio, where we have relatives and German-speaking friends."

Out of deference to the Schmidt family, James and Hedwig settled in Dayton, Ohio. They were among German-speaking craftsmen and skilled trades people like themselves, all looking for a better life.

James liked this new land, so full of opportunities. He studied English in night school and worked for a furniture manufacturer ten hours each day, six days per week. Hedwig became pregnant with their first child and longed for the company of her mother. With James working so many hours and going to night school, she became very homesick and decided to have her baby delivered by a midwife in her parents' home in Kutina, Austria-Hungary.

On one of the few evenings when James came home for supper before going to night school, she asked, "Would you mind terribly if I visited with my parents and had our baby delivered by my family's midwife? You work all day and go to school at night. I hardly see you anymore."

James knew Hedwig was homesick and missed her parents, but he defended himself, saying, "I am trying to provide a better life for us and our children. I am learning English and my paycheck is increasing. Everything is getting better. I thought that was what you wanted?" he asked, feeling somewhat hurt.

"It is," she replied, "but I am home alone all day with not much to do. I would feel so much better to have my mother help with the baby."

James loved Hedwig and understood her need to see her parents again and have her mother near during delivery. He knew he would miss her but agreed, feeling he would build their income during her absence and provide a better home upon her return with their new baby.

Hedwig, seven months pregnant, traveled alone back to Europe, first by train to New York, and then by ship across the Atlantic, through the Mediterranean, to Trieste, Italy. From there, it was a five-hour train ride to Kutina, in Austria-Hungary. Her journey took fourteen days.

Five months later, she returned to Dayton with their new three-month-old daughter, Rose. James was beaming with pride. He found a nicely furnished apartment, had a secure job, and felt that he would provide well for his budding family. Hedwig, feeling content, became a homemaker, saved their money diligently, and tended to their beautiful daughter.

Two years later, Hedwig and James were blessed with the birth of a son. They named him James, after his father. Unfortunately, he developed a medical condition by age two. A weakness in his legs prevented him from standing without help. An older German doctor recommended a change of climate. Hedwig insisted on going back to Europe. James, who had a good job with a bright future, was reluctant to leave. "Why do you wish to go back?" he asked.

"I miss my family but also feel that the fresh clean air from the farmlands around Kutina will help Jimmy grow stronger."

For the time being, they stayed in Dayton and hoped for the best for little Jimmy. By now, Rose was a feisty, energetic five-year-old with dark hair and large brown eyes.

A devastating flood of the Miami River changed their lives. Many homes and livestock were washed away by the rising water, including the furniture plant where James worked and the apartment they rented.

Hedwig saved herself and her two children by jumping into an empty row boat that was drifting by their apartment. There were no oars, and she drifted downstream for several miles before she was rescued.

James was working on the opposite side of the river when the flood struck. He and others ran to higher ground just in time to watch their small factory disappear into the turbulent river. The Kousak family did not have insurance, and their future suddenly looked dim. They were thankful just to be together and alive.

Due to their desperate economic condition, James and Hedwig decided to return to Europe with their two children. They traveled to Kutina, where Hedwig's parents had their brick manufacturing business. The business climate was still good in this part of Austria-Hungary, and the political climate seemed to be stable, at least more so than farther south and east.

James became involved in roofing tile manufacturing at the insistence of the Schmidt family. He would have preferred cabinetmaking but deferred to Hedwig's parents, feeling he had somehow failed her in the United States.

They told him that he would be a business owner like them and that roofing tiles would complement their brick manufacturing and it would all be a successful family-owned business. At first, James was doubtful, wishing to work with wood, building cabinets, but, at Hedwig's urging, he decided to give this new venture a try and keep peace in the family. All seemed well until he was abruptly drafted into the Austrian army to fight a budding war in Montenegro, to the south, where insurgents demanded independence from Austria-Hungary.

After a three-month stint, order was restored, and James returned to his family. He knew that political unrest was spreading north and would soon escalate into something much bigger.

He said to Hedwig, "We must return to the United States where we can raise our family without the fear of war. It's only a matter of time before the empire erupts. There is too much political unrest."

She hated the thought of leaving her parents, the social life she was becoming accustomed to, and the business that James was building with her family's help. However, being pragmatic and thinking that perhaps he was right, she suggested, "Why don't you go first before they draft you into the army again. You can find a nice place for us to live, and I'll follow as soon as I receive your letter."

James left for Dayton, Ohio, despondent about having to leave his family behind, but he thought he would be able to build a nice nest egg before they arrived.

He knew Hedwig hated to leave her parents and the comfort of her homeland. Hedwig and her parents placed great hope in Emperor Franz Joseph's ability to keep Austria-Hungary at peace.

Before James left for Dayton, Hedwig became pregnant once again. She sent the good news to relatives in Dayton to tell James that he needed to build a new crib and that she was going to remain in Kutina until the baby was born. This time, she gave birth to another baby girl. She named her Josephine.

The mail at times was unpredictable, and the news never reached James. He did not have any trouble finding a job. His old employer rebuilt the furniture factory and needed his woodworking skills. James knew of the expanding political problems in Europe and sent several letters to Hedwig, pleading with her to bring their family to Dayton.

The date was October 1913, and a terrible depression was sweeping across Europe. Hedwig's requests for immigration to the United States were denied. She did not receive James's letters, and the lack of news from her husband made the situation all the more desperate for her.

Her family's business fell into insolvency; prices were skyrocketing. She moved her children into her parents' large home, but even there, her parents were forced to rent out six rooms to make ends meet.

All the armies of Europe were mobilizing. The Central Powers, consisting of Germany, Austria Hungary, Bulgaria, and the Ottoman Empire, were opposed by the Allies, consisting of France, England, Russia, and later the United States.

Hedwig was determined to take her family to the United States and pleaded with the government to let her go. She did not understand why she had not received any news from James by now and assumed that he was still in Dayton. She waited daily for mail from the government granting her permission to emigrate and for news from James.

After writing a letter to a relative in Dayton, she received a reply stating, "Since James never received an answer from all his letters to you over the past year, he became brokenhearted and assumed you found someone else. He left Dayton for Detroit, where he found work at a Detroit motor company." But nobody knew which motor company James was employed by, compounding their problem.

Hedwig finally received a letter from the Austrian government requesting her to travel to Prague to receive her passport for America. The reasoning was that since she married James, who was a Bohemian, she needed to travel to Prague, the capital of Bohemia, for her papers.

Hedwig, with her three children, Rose, Jimmy, and young Josephine, traveled to Prague, received their passports, and traveled by train to Rotterdam. There, they waited to board the last steamship to the United States just before the beginning of World War I. The docks along the Rotterdam waterfront were filled with families wishing to flee the imminent war. All the benches along the wharf were full of sleeping children and parents, some of whom were waiting for days to board a ship to America. Hedwig found the situation deplorable. She found out that their ship would not depart until the next day and refused to have her children sleep on a dockside bench.

She carried with her a pail of twenty pork chops, ensconced in pork fat to keep them fresh, and covered with a cloth. With this pail of pork chops, she approached a harbor official.

"Dear Sir, would you be able to provide overnight lodging for myself and my children in exchange for these fresh pork chops?" She showed him the uncovered pail.

Good food was scarce, and he was an understanding man. "Madam, it will be my pleasure to have you stay at our home tonight. My wife loves children and will be happy to meet you. We have two daughters and five grandchildren, but they all moved to America several years ago. They write us often, but it isn't like seeing them. My work will be finished by 6:00 PM, and our apartment is near."

True to his word, his wife was delighted to meet Hedwig and the children. She cooked potatoes and sauerkraut, which she served with the pork chops. After dinner, his wife insisted that Hedwig and the children sleep in their bed while she and her husband slept on a couch.

The next day, after a restful night, Hedwig and her children boarded the last steamship to leave Rotterdam for the United States. Two days later, on August 4th, 1914, German troops crossed the Belgian border; World War I began.

When they arrived in the United States, they traveled to Detroit, Michigan, to the last address they had for James. After many inquiries, Hedwig was told that James had moved on to Saginaw, Michigan, where he was employed in the model department at the Erdman & Guider Co., builders of trucks, owned by Graham Paige. She called the Erdman & Guider Company and requested James Kousak's address.

The personnel manager was impressed by Hedwig's determination and sent a message to James. "Your family will arrive on the 5:00 PM Greyhound bus tomorrow."

Receiving this news, James was stunned. *What family?* he wondered. *Will I recognize them?* He thought for sure that his wife and family were gone forever.

When the bus arrived in Saginaw, a tall, slim man in his early thirties jumped inside the open door. Hedwig, recognizing her husband, stood up from her seat and cried out "Jim!"

The man dashed by surprised passengers and threw his lanky arms around Hedwig, crying, "Thank God you are alive and here."

Rose, Jimmy, and Josephine, feeling their mother's emotion, began crying from joy. Their father took all three in his arms and hugged them, saying, "My beautiful children. Look how tall you have grown."

Josephine was the youngest. She didn't know her father and tried to pull away. He looked at her in surprise, gave her a kiss on the cheek, and said, "You are as pretty as your mother." That did it. She warmed up, realizing that this cheerful man was her dad.

James did, however, wonder why Hedwig did not respond to his many letters. He needed to have a serious discussion with her, to clear the air.

"Why didn't you respond to my letters requesting you to join me in Dayton? I had a furnished apartment ready for our family."

"There was a depression. All the armies were mobilizing. My family lost everything. Mail was not getting through," she responded tearfully. "I traveled to Prague in order to obtain our passport. Our mail must have been lost in the malaise of political unrest and all the migrating we both did."

James heard that conditions were very bad in Europe and that war was breaking out. He realized it was a miracle that his wife and children were able to get out and was overjoyed they were together as a family once again. Little did they know that a similar episode would be repeated years later?

James lived in a one-bedroom apartment and knew it was too small for his family of five. They managed for a few days with two extra mattresses, but at week's end, James surprised Hedwig by putting a down payment on a two-story, three-bedroom, white frame house.

The front porch was sagging, some of the windows were cracked and needed replacing, and the plumbing needed fixing, but James was up to the task and soon turned it into a very livable home for the whole family.

Rose and Jimmy were enrolled in a nearby Saginaw elementary school in September of 1914. They assimilated quickly and enjoyed playing with all their new friends. There was, however, an episode in the third grade when some of the bigger boys would not allow her brother Jimmy, who was in the first grade, to go to the bathroom. She saw him come out, ashamed of himself, with wet pants and tears in his eyes.

Infuriated, she ran into the boys' bathroom, surprising the boys inside. "Which one of you didn't let my brother relieve himself?" she demanded.

Surprised at seeing a very angry girl in their bathroom, none of the boys wanted to take the blame. One of the biggest laughed, saying, "Too bad he couldn't hold it!" Infuriated, Rose walked up to him and punched him in the nose with all her might.

Frightened, the boys ran out into the hall, followed by their leader, who was crying now and holding a hand over his bloody nose. Rose ran after them, yelling, "You bunch of cowards. Leave my brother alone!" Later that day, Rose received a reprimand from the principal.

Hedwig found out several hours later that she had a headstrong tomboy for a daughter. Little Jimmy never had another problem, and Rose was given a wide berth of respect by the older boys.

James Kousak received another promotion and was asked to transfer to Highland Park, Michigan, where he supervised the modeling department in what was now the Chrysler Motor Company. Erdman & Guider became Dodge Motors, which in turn became Chrysler. The Kousak family found a house on Rhode Island Street in Highland Park, within walking distance of the new Chrysler headquarters.

Remembering that story gave Rose the willpower and determination to find a way out of Prague and save her family. *My mother did it, and I will too! There must be a way out, and I will find it!* she thought, marshaling her energies.

Josephine and Paul's last attempt to help Rose.

Chapter 11

Always bear in mind that your own resolution
to succeed is more important than any other
one thing.

--Abraham Lincoln

The date was May 1949; weeks had passed since Rose received any news. She felt desolate and wondered if anyone was trying to help her. She had not received any information since her last letter to her sister Josephine and was unaware of the efforts being made on her behalf.

In the meantime, Josephine and her husband Paul did their best to help her through their contact with Senator Vandenberg's office, but it was to no avail. To complicate things further and add more sorrow to their situation, Rose received news from the American consul's office of a telegram sent to Anthony in Switzerland from her brother-in-law in Reed City, Michigan:

Exhausted all sources for help. Impossible to get passport for Rose. Any additional activity on our part will jeopardize your family's personal safety.

Paul Ivkovich.

A month passed without results, and Rose decided on another plan.

She heard through friends that in an area close to the West German border, just north of Austria, Czechs who were still loyal to the Benes government helped families escape. Unable to go herself and not wishing to arouse suspicion, she sent her daughter Zdenka on a scouting mission to see if there was such a possibility. "I am asking you to do something very brave and very important," she told Zdenka. "I want you to travel to Modrava and inquire about the possibility of hiring a guide. If he asks why we need him, tell him for hiking or hunting."

Zdenka was worried and asked, "What if I find such a person, and he asks where my parents are? What then?"

"Just write his name and telephone number down and tell him that I will contact him in the near future," replied Rose, wondering if she was asking too much of her teenage daughter, hoping she wasn't placing her in danger. She decided it had to be done.

Zdenka, an intelligent sixteen-year-old, felt proud of her mother's trust. She took the train to Modrava, a village within eighteen miles of the West German border. It was one of the larger villages in Sumova (Bohemian Forest), a heavily wooded, hilly area. It stretched north from Austria along the German-Czech border, through many miles of unspoiled nature known for its clean, crisp, therapeutic air. At sixteen, Zdenka didn't arouse suspicion in the border area. The train arrived near noon.

Zdenka was hungry by now and asked the conductor, "Pardon me, sir, is there a restaurant nearby?"

"Yes," he replied, "the one in the village square directly down the street from the train station is a good one. The people are friendly, and the food is good. Try the potato salad with kielbasa. It's my favorite."

She thanked him and walked towards the restaurant, worried about how she would find a guide. *Who do I ask? How do I make inquiries?* She wondered. She was frightened inside, not knowing exactly what was expected of her, but tried to look as brave and inconspicuous as possible.

The day was clear and luminous, and the sidewalk in front of the restaurant was filled with local people eating their lunches and drinking their coffee or beer. They were sitting on wooden stools, around quaint wooden tables; it was a picturesque country setting. *How peaceful it all looks*, Zdenka thought, feeling a little better about her mission. She sat at an outdoor table and ordered kielbasa with potato salad, a local dish. The food helped settle the butterflies in her stomach.

When she finished eating, she asked the waitress, "Do you know of any guides who take people hunting or hiking?"

"I do not," she replied, "but why don't you ask some of the local people sitting nearby?"

Zdenka thanked her and asked one of the men sitting at a table next to her. The man just finished his beer and looked at her curiously. "Why is a young girl like you looking for a guide? Do you plan on going hunting?" he asked laughingly.

"No, but I will be coming back with my mother and father. We like to hike and would like a guide, at least for the first day, to familiarize ourselves with your beautiful surroundings."

"In that case, I suggest Slava, the local woodcutter. He is a good man and guides tourists and hunters in his spare time. He lives over there," he said, pointing at a small thatched roof house, a short distance away.

"Thank you," Zdenka answered. She finished her lunch and walked over to the guide's home.

She knocked on the door and was met by a large, elderly man with a weathered face, probably from many years spent outdoors. He had bushy white hair and a well-trimmed, white beard, and he looked honest and fatherly to her.

"Come in!" he said with a wide smile.

"Are you Mr. Slava?" Zdenka asked, hesitating in the doorway.

"Yes, I am Slava. Come in. It's not every day that I meet a pretty young lady."

Zdenka decided to stand in the doorway. He seemed overly friendly.

Noticing Zdenka's uncertainty, he tried putting her at ease, saying, "I am a widower of many years. I lost two sons in the war but have three daughters, who blessed me with five grandchildren. They visit me often and help me clean up this place."

Zdenka noticed that the inside of the cabin looked freshly swept but instinct told her to speak with him in the opened doorway.

"I don't blame you," he quipped. "These days you should not trust anyone, not even an old geezer like me. Maybe if my daughters were more careful like you, I wouldn't have so many grandchildren."

It was an offhand remark that left Zdenka with mixed feelings. *Is he trustworthy?* she wondered. *Did his daughters have children out of wedlock? Why tell me?* Quickly dismissing those thoughts as silly, she said, "My parents would be interested in hiring you for a hiking trip."

He nodded his head and said, "For a fee, I have guided many hunters looking for deer and elk. I rescued lost hunters and hikers all over these mountains for years and would be happy to guide your family."

He gave Zdenka his name and the telephone number of the nearby courthouse, saying, "They will notify me when your parents call. Have them call me through the courthouse number. I don't have a telephone in my house. It's much too expensive. Most of the people in this village receive their calls through the courthouse." She thanked him and boarded the next train back to Prague.

Zdenka returned unharmed, proud of the information she obtained. Rose followed up with inquires. She left a message at the courthouse, and a week later, met the guide in a Prague cafe.

She recognized him by Zdenka's description: a big man with a white beard. By the tone of his voice and his independent attitude, he appeared to be an anti-Communist and a pro-Benes sympathizer. Rose felt she could trust him and decided to tell him her plans.

Upon hearing her story and noticing she was an American, he cited the danger and asked for one hundred American dollars to be paid up front. Noticing her unease, he said, "Kind madam, you must understand that I need to pay border guards and buy provisions to make your trip successful."

Rose felt she didn't have much choice and decided to pay him. "I hope I can trust you. I have no one else to turn to for help."

"Don't worry, madam. I am not a Communist. I am a free man. Nobody tells me what to do!"

They decided to meet October 11th, 1949, in the restaurant of an inn close to the border. Her problem now was how to receive government permission to travel to a restricted border area and avoid suspicion.

Once again, she asked Dr. Hnevkovsky for help. "Dear doctor, I need your help once more. I must have permission to be able to travel to the Modrava Inn, near the border. It is our only hope for escape," she pleaded.

The good doctor knew their situation well and promised to help in any way possible. He remembered the extra beeswax penicillin the Kozaks allowed him to keep following Jaroslav's release from the sanitarium and the large box of antibiotics, unavailable in Prague that Anthony recently sent from Switzerland, in gratitude for helping Jaroslav. He vowed to help the Kozak family reunite in the West.

Rose was sitting in a large, leather, wing-backed chair, facing the doctor's desk, just to the right of the door to his office, feeling grateful for his willingness to help, when the door suddenly burst open.

A large, rough-looking man rushed in with outstretched arms, shouting in a booming voice, "Comrade Doctor, I am well enough to return to work for our new government, thanks to you." He reached across the desk and vigorously shook the startled doctor's hand. "It's all that we worked and hoped for isn't it?" he continued loudly. "We finally replaced all those blood-sucking capitalists with hardworking Czechs, loyal to the Party. It's a glorious day for Communism! "

Rose did her best not to be noticed, slouching deep in the large lounger, partly hidden by the open door, as he abruptly walked out. Hearing all this, she tried hard to make herself invisible and breathed a sigh of relief when he left.

"I apologize for this unfortunate incident," Dr. Hnevkovsky said to Rose, noticing her concern. "I hope you took a good look at that character. His name is Dominic Hruby, a ruthless Communist thug, totally dedicated to the Party. He works as hired muscle for the secret police, apprehending defectors wherever they are. We were in a concentration camp together during the Nazi occupation." Noticing the concerned look on Rose's face, he quickly said. "Don't worry; I have nothing to do with him or his kind. I heard that two of my assistants crossed the border through the Bohemian Forest, close to where you wish to go. I do not need to know your plan, but whatever you do, do not trust anyone, not even your best friends. There are informers everywhere. These are dangerous times, Mrs. Kozak. May our Lord guide you safely. I will write a letter to the Ministry of Interior, recommending long walks in the healing air of the Bohemian Forest for Jaroslav's recovery."

Europeans, in general, believed in the recuperative powers of exercise in clean mountain air. The Communists were no exception. Besides, they didn't believe a forty-two-year-old woman, her daughter, and her crippled son would attempt an eighteen-mile defection through some of the wildest parts of the country into West Germany—especially since the inn where they were allowed to stay was a half-mile below a border guard barracks!

Permission was granted, and Rose was given a document of free passage. Rose quickly sent a deceptive telegram to Anthony, which read:

My dearest Anthony, a friend of Senator Vandenberg came to Prague, intervened on our behalf with the Ministry of Interior, and obtained permission for us to travel to Switzerland. The Czech authorities, at the last minute, decided that families should stay together. All of this will only take a few more weeks, to process the papers. The miracle we all prayed for has finally happened. Soon we will be reunited in the West. Please, I beg you, do not return to Prague.

It was another fib to keep Anthony from returning to Prague. The message was sent through the American Consulate, which was closed soon after by order of the new Communist government under Premier Klement Gottwald.

Before departing, Rose decided to make a short trip to Karlovy Vary, a resort city near the West German border known for its therapeutic baths, in an attempt to sell some of her crystal to a distant relative who lived there. She carefully packed a vase, six wine goblets, and two large serving plates into her rucksack. It would only be a one-hour train ride, she surmised, and she planned to be back before Jaroslav and Zdenka came home from school. At nine o'clock the next the morning, she boarded the train, set her rucksack under her seat, made herself comfortable, and started to read a newspaper, catching up on all the political problems facing Prague. As the train rolled along, she became aware of a heated conversation between four men in the next cubicle of seats. One of the men, with a familiar voice, said, "When we catch this next group of traitors, we should have a public execution in Karlovy Vary. That will discourage all the others from escaping into West Germany!"

"But, Dom," the other man said, "our orders are to detain them and hold them for questioning. The police want to find out who their guides are and who is getting paid off."

"Don't be stupid!" exclaimed Dom. "I have done this before, and the best therapy to stop these bourgeoisie parasites from escaping is to set an example by shooting them in public. Believe me, word will spread and that will put an end to anyone escaping in this area. Once we finish here, we will move to another area along the border and do the same until the entire border with West Germany is secure! Our comrades in the government will be happy with our results!"

Rose knew she heard that voice before. She slowly looked over the top of her newspaper and recognized Dominic Hruby, the thug who was in Dr. Hnevkovsky's office. Fear gripped her. She had to get off the train.

At the next stop, she quickly stood up, pulled the rucksack out from under her seat, and started to strap it on her back, when a gruff voice behind her said, "Let me help you." Before she could react, a hand pulled the rucksack up onto her back. "An attractive woman like you should not have to lift such a heavy rucksack." To her consternation, it was Hruby! "You look worried," he said. "Is something wrong?"

"There is nothing wrong," she wheezed, keeping her head down, hoping she wasn't recognized. She pulled away from him and quickly stepped off the train and returned to Prague with the rucksack full of crystal. There was no way she would take the chance of getting off the train with those brutal men in Karlovy Vary, and be recognized. She returned home before the kids returned from school and decided to leave the crystal there.

June 1949. Last photo of family sent to Anthony in Switzerland.

Chapter 12

If the freedom of speech is taken away
then dumb and silent we may be led,
like sheep to the slaughter.

--George Washington

The October 11th date was approaching, and Rose hurried to get her affairs in order. Since Anthony wasn't there to help, she relied heavily on Zdenka to help prepare for the escape.

Jaroslav was aware that something unusual was happening, but no one told him anything for fear he may say something to his playmates that would arouse suspicion. Secrecy was the key! Whenever he asked questions, Rose and Zdenka just answered vaguely that they were planning a short vacation to a nearby resort.

Rose fabricated stories for curious friends, telling them they were going to a health resort in the mountains where long walks were prescribed by government doctors for Jaroslav's recovery and that they would return in a couple of weeks. It was a show of bravado. In truth, she was very worried, placing the trust of her family and the little money she had into the hands of a guide she didn't know.

She wondered what she would do if he didn't show up and confided her fears to Zdenka, a pragmatic sixteen-year-old with Girl Scout training.

"If this fails, your father will be forced to return, and we will suffer dire consequences at the hands of this government."

"Don't worry, Mother; the guide looked trustworthy. He told me he was a grandfather with many grandchildren," Zdenka replied. She was troubled, not knowing how to soothe her mother's feelings. "He seemed willing to help us and knows the countryside well." She hoped all that was true.

Zdenka decided to cut out a section of a map illustrating the border area they planned to visit. The piece was small, but it highlighted the topography, which detailed the German-Czech border, the roads, and the fire trails crossing it. She folded this map carefully and placed it into a hollowed area she carved out of the heel of her left shoe. She didn't tell anyone, deciding it was insurance in case things turned bad. She carefully tacked the heel back into place and walked with an air of self-confidence, knowing she would be able to help her mother in case the map was needed.

Zdenka was brimming with responsibility and was gratified that her mother confided in her, but, deep inside, she was frightened by the awesome risk they faced. She wasn't afraid of the woods, having camped overnight with the Girl Scouts on many occasions, but nevertheless, foreboding thoughts raced through her mind. She asked herself what would happen if the guide didn't show up. She remembered her suspicions. If he did show up, was he honest or was he working for the Communists, turning in escapees, like some of the stories she had heard? What would happen if they were caught? Would her mother be deported without her and Jaroslav? Would her father return to help them or would they all be separated for life? Would she and Jaroslav be split-up if adopted by a Communist family? She tried her best to keep up a brave front as she secretly longed for the security of her parents' arms wrapped around her.

Seven-year-old Jaroslav didn't have such thoughts. He didn't know what was going on. It was just as well, because at his age, he would not have understood anyway. He missed his dad but was happy they were going on vacation and he didn't have to go to school. He wasn't well enough to play soccer or hockey like his school friends, so he was just glad to get away from the teasing and the constant adulation of the Russian Army. He heard his parents discuss American victories and the air battles over England. *Why don't they discuss the air battles over England in school?* he thought. *Didn't the Americans do anything like Mom said?* He decided not to say anything in school but knew there was more to this than what he was told. The Allies of the West were never discussed in his school, only Russian victories.

The days became shorter, nighttime approached sooner, and the warmth from the afternoon sun soon lost ground to the brisk October air. Winds were picking up, and the rustling of falling leaves suggested the approach of an early winter.

Chapter 13

*We confide in our strength, without
boasting of it; we respect that of others,
without fearing it.*

--Thomas Jefferson

One afternoon, while the children were in school, Rose received a visit from Anthony's business associate, Jan Svetensko. The Svetenskos had been friends of the Kozaks for a number of years, and Rose didn't notice anything out of the ordinary, except for the fact that he came alone. In the past, whenever they visited, it was always a family gathering with wives and children. She remembered Anthony's warning that Svetensko would probably have turned Communist.

Jan Svetensko came in with a big smile and a friendly greeting. Although suspicious of the visit and remembering Anthony's warning, Rose remained cordial. She served coffee and *parnicky* (home-baked cookies), as custom dictated. *Why now?* she wondered. His handshake was cold and damp; his gestures seemed insincere.

At first, they exchanged pleasantries and spoke mainly about their families. Soon, however, Mr. Svetensko asked Rose, "How does Anthony feel about the new Gottwald government?"

Rose, surprised but instantly alert, replied, "Why don't you ask him? He will be home soon." She was well aware how friends informed on friends during this precarious time and asked, "Mr. Svetensko, we have known each other's families for ten years and never discussed politics. Why now?"

"I wish to help Anthony," he replied, "so the new government will view him favorably when he returns from Switzerland to defend himself against those false charges."

Rose, suspicious by now, asked, "How would you know how the government feels about my husband and why would it matter to you?"

He shook his head sadly and remonstrated, "The Communists regard anyone who is not a member of the Party as a subversive. I have friends in high places and can help Anthony. We have been friends for a long time, and I wish to help him."

He placed his hand on her knee and looked longingly into her eyes. She pulled away thinking, *Not with me, you lascivious creep! You're more like a fiend than a friend.* He disgusted her. She knew he had always been envious of Anthony's work and would like nothing better than to take over his department. He never acquired Anthony's language skills or his knowledge of international tariffs but now saw a political opportunity to expose Anthony as a Benes sympathizer and thus hoped to deliver the fatal stroke to his career. She knew it would come to that soon: first Komarek and now Svetensko, another Judas.

She needed more time and cleverly responded, "Mr. Svetensko, you know I am not political and cannot speak for Anthony. Why don't you ask him when he returns? He has always been a loyal Czech. Why should he feel any different now?"

"Times have changed!" he replied brusquely, standing up to leave. He looked around, smiling sardonically. As he put on his coat, he remarked, "You have a beautiful residence; hopefully, the government will look at Anthony favorably and allow you to keep it." With that, he walked out the door.

His last words sent a chill down her back and made her realize she better sell as many possessions as possible before they confiscated everything.

Three days later, long after the children went to bed, Rose was busy writing down an inventory of possessions she planned to sell. There was a sudden knock at the front door. She wondered who would come at this late hour, rising out of her chair and walking to the door with mounting fear. She slowly opened the door to the length of the chain lock and peered out at two men in dark coats.

"Who are you and what do you want at this late hour?" she asked.

"Police," said the taller one. "We must ask you for important information. Let us in. We will not harm you." They showed their identification. Rose, very frightened, unlocked the door, knowing they would break it down if she refused. They quickly entered, wanting to know where Anthony was.

"Where is your husband?" they demanded, and began searching the rooms. One walked into the kitchen, the other into the living room, both very brusque and without consideration for Rose's feelings.

This is Svetensko's doing, thought Rose. *He is trying to scare me through his government friends. He was always a manipulator*, she remembered, *always seeking to exploit a perceived weakness in others.*

When they came to the children's room, Rose rushed to the closed door and defiantly retorted, "Don't you dare enter my daughter's bedroom if you have any sense of decency left in you!" With blazing eyes, she stood her ground. "You have no right to intimidate me and my family! My husband is returning soon, and the Ministry of Interior is aware of that. Now, please leave! I am an American and shall report this outrage to my friend Mr. Slepak at the Ministry of Interior."

Both men stared at her in astonishment, not used to such an audacious outburst from a woman. They appeared to be in their early thirties. One was short with broad shoulders, slanted eyes, dark hair, and prominent Mongolian cheek bones, while the other was tall and slim with blond hair. The tall one looked at the table, saw the itemized list, and asked, "What are you planning to do with this list of possessions?"

"I'm hoping to sell everything on the list," she replied, "to pay for my son's medical bills." Although it wasn't the whole truth, it was believable. They apologized for any inconvenience and left.

By the end of the following week, she sold their grand piano and other fine furniture to neighbors and friends at very reasonable prices. She gave her Bohemian crystal, Anthony's cameras, and books to a cousin, hoping that someday they may be returned. She felt reasonably assured that she had enough extra money to meet any emergencies that might come up.

A decision to escape was made. Rose confided in Zdenka, "My darling, your father isn't here; I am depending on your courage and your Girl Scout training. I cannot do this alone and need your help. We must leave soon."

Zdenka was shook up. She didn't know exactly what her mother expected of her, and the uncertainty troubled her. However, she knew the country was in political turmoil and that her mother was right. They had to leave. So, whatever needed to be done, she would do her best.

Rose hoped she had made the right decision. There was no one to trust, nobody to turn to for help. The American Embassy, for reasons she still did not understand, refused to help and the Tygarts from the consulate office left for the United States weeks before. She knew that something wasn't right. Her passport had somehow disappeared. She knew that passports were highly prized on the black market and commanded a high price. She remembered having to give it up months before, at the request of the new Communist government. Now they denied ever having it. Her birth certificate also disappeared. She searched her mind and thought that perhaps it may have been stolen the night the two policemen came to her home inquiring about Anthony. She remembered all the documents on her table and the inventory list of items she wanted to sell. *Was my birth certificate on the table?* she wondered. She returned to the Czech administration office, but the young clerk there denied ever having it. She was hoping that someone at the U.S. Embassy could help her, but once again, it was to no avail. A few days later, she heard that it was closing down. Some of the employees were Czech and probably Communists. Instinct told her to be very careful.

Rose was despondent and felt terribly alone. There was no one to turn to for help. She knew she deceived Anthony and that her only chance to save her family was to escape. She remembered how her mother overcame her problems and united her family, and knew that she must do the same. Her plan was marginal at best, but it was the only one she had. To hesitate longer would increase their danger. It was time to act.

Did anyone suspect our plan to escape? How did I get myself and my family into this predicament? she lamented. She thought of the courage her mother must have had crossing the Atlantic Ocean those numerous times before the outbreak of World War I. She thought of the trials her parents endured and overcame. With a heavy heart, she prayed into the night, "Please, Lord, give me the courage my mother had. Help me to reunite my family the way she did."

Chapter 14

Love your neighbor, but don't
pull down your hedge.

--Benjamin Franklin

On October 8th, 1949, Rose, Zdenka, and Jaroslav boarded a steam-driven train to Modrava, a village approximately eighteen miles from the West German border. Hours later, the sparsely occupied train, with only the Kozaks and a few soldiers, arrived at its destination. Rose and Zdenka strapped their tightly packed rucksacks to their backs, grabbed Jaroslav by the hands, and stepped off the train to the hissing sound of steam being released from the locomotive. It was an overcast day with a light drizzle.

A group of soldiers stepping off the train called jovial greetings to Zdenka. "Hi, beautiful. How about a date? We're in the barracks up the hill from the inn," they joked. Zdenka, her cheeks flushed, beamed with all the attention.

Rose did not think it was funny. She gave them an icy glare and said, "Where are your manners? Is this the way your parents raised you?!" The young men hurried ahead, red-faced and silent.

Zdenka remembered the place where she found the guide. Modrava was a picturesque village nestled in the foothills of the Bohemian Forest, the last village this close to the West German border. In another time, it would teem with tourists, but now it looked desolate, devoid of children or families. The inn stood on the banks of a fast flowing river, a quarter mile west of the village.

ntal note to check her map to see if this river crossed
he importance of having several reference points to
nn felt good after their tiring train ride.

his wife greeted them warmly. "Welcome, Mrs.
aid. "We received a letter from the Ministry of
ing your visit with your two children. Please enjoy

...nank you," Rose replied. She knew they would be watched and made
a mental note to be steadfast and careful.

It was an old building with ten rooms, five upstairs and five down, with
a common bathroom at the end of each hallway. There was a kitchen and
dining room on the lower level. Rose was surprised when the innkeeper
showed them their second-floor room. It was large, with three single beds
covered with down feather quilts. There was a wooden table with chairs in
the middle of the room and a heavy oak wardrobe in a corner, next to which
was a wash basin with soap and a large pitcher of water underneath. Clean
towels hung on a wooden rack. The wood floor was freshly scrubbed, and
clean hand-woven throw rugs were placed next to each bed. She opened a
large window to let the fresh air in and looked out across a swiftly flowing
river. Cows were grazing in a large bowl-shaped meadow, surrounded by a
pine forest, which reached into the rolling hills beyond.

Rose took a deep breath of fresh air, feeling invigorated. She said to
Zdenka and Jaroslav, "This is a wonderful place, miles away from the city,
with its depressing politics and polluted air. We will all be rejuvenated, and
I sense that good fortune will follow." Both Zdenka and Jaroslav felt their
mother's enthusiasm and hoped her prediction was right.

The inn had been government-owned since the Communist takeover.
The couple who managed it took turns cooking daily meals for the military
personnel from nearby barracks.

This area was restricted to tourists, and all of the necessary documents
allowing the Kozaks to stay had been forwarded to the innkeeper, who
was told to watch for any suspicious behavior. Rose, Zdenka, and Jaroslav
awakened early each morning, packed sandwiches into their knapsack, filled
two canteens with water, and went on their daily hike.

The innkeeper said to Rose, "Please take my dog with you on your walks.
The countryside is a wilderness, and the dog knows his way back in case you
become lost."

As long as they take the dog, they will not try to escape, the innkeeper
thought, remembering other Czechs who escaped into Germany through this
area in the past year. The dog always returned home when he got hungry.
Besides, dogs bark and run around, making them easy to track. On the other

hand, security has tightened and he remembered that the escapees were all men. This woman and her kids shouldn't be a problem.

Rose knew they only had two days to familiarize themselves with the area before her meeting with the guide on October 11th. She had a nagging feeling in the back of her mind that something would go wrong. She now wished she had not paid him in advance and prayed he would show up. She knew all their moves were monitored by the innkeeper and his wife, and took extra care to look like a concerned parent who was only there to help her son recover from his illness.

Rose was undaunted; she knew this was the only way out. Of course, she was concerned over Jaroslav, but she also knew that using his illness was the subterfuge needed for their escape. All of her options were exhausted. For two days, they took long hikes along trails deemed safe. The innkeeper explained to Rose, "Mrs. Kozak, this is a government-restricted area. You must pay attention to the danger signs along the trail. There are old German signs warning of the border zone. The signs read '*Grenze-Verboten*' meaning the border is near and it is a forbidden area to enter. Now that I told you what the signs mean there will be no excuse for not knowing."

"Thank you. I will try to remember that," Rose replied, thinking, *What a country bumpkin. At least now I know we are close.* But she also knew that they had to be careful not to be caught in the restricted area. To be caught crossing into this area would mean a fast trip back to Prague and an end to their chance for escape.

The countryside was beautiful, with serpentine trails snaking their way up colorful hillsides, only to disappear, a mere wisp, into the dark forest. Fall colors of red, yellow, and brown were distinct in the hazy afternoon sunshine. Leaves falling from stately oaks, maples, and lindens, scattered across the countryside in the cool breeze. Sunlight penetrating through a light blue sky reflected off the waters of swift-flowing mountain streams, etching out the valleys below. Old weatherworn wooden Stations of the Cross marked the trail every mile or so, most likely built during the Hapsburg dynasty. They stood on four-foot pilings and had small, protective, tent-shaped overhangs across their top. Each station had a wooden drawer built under the carving of Christ. These drawers were used for notes from passing hikers wishing to express their thoughts. Rose whispered a prayer asking for divine guidance. As they approached one particular Station of the Cross, they had a panoramic view over a sloping valley. On the opposite hillside, they noticed an observation tower and a wide firebreak cutting a swath westward through the forest. Zdenka, with her keen vision, noticing it first, said to Rose, "Mother, that firebreak heads in a westerly direction and may cross into

Germany. Some of those firebreaks stretch for miles. It is possible that this one may extend over the border."

"You may be right," Rose replied, looking across the valley. "Now would be the perfect time to check our map to see just how far it extends." She looked into her bag and realized she left the map in her suitcase in their room.

"Mother, I have a map in my shoe," Zdenka confessed seeing the distressed look on Rose's face. She removed her left shoe, took off the heel, and proudly pulled out a small map. They studied the map and noticed that the firebreak crossed into West Germany. A plan began to gel. Jaroslav occupied himself by flinging rocks down the hillside. The old dog they took along, tired of chasing Jaroslav's rocks, flopped next to the trail with his tongue hanging out. Jaroslav pretended the rocks were hand grenades and threw them with relish at invisible enemies climbing up the hill; he was an energetic seven-year-old testing the limits of his war-inspired imagination.

In the meantime, Rose and Zdenka decided they found the correct firebreak. Zdenka marked the map and decided to use the observation tower as a possible landmark if it became necessary.

Rose chastised Zdenka for the risk she took hiding the map in the heel of her shoe. "What if," Rose asked, "you decided to wear a different pair of shoes and someone searched our room during our absence and discovered your makeshift heel? The consequences would be dire." Noticing Zdenka's disappointment, she said, "I'm sorry. I know you meant well. You prepared yourself skillfully, but we must be very careful not to let your map fall into wrong hands. The large map of Czechoslovakia that I left in the suitcase would not raise suspicion like this small one of just this section of the border area."

On their return hike in the ebbing sunshine, they noticed a purplish-blue haze drifting up from the valleys over neighboring hillsides, confirming the approaching October nightfall. The Kozak family hurried back to the inn. Rose, Zdenka, Jaroslav, and the dog returned just in time for dinner.

They found the dining room filled with noisy, beer-drinking border guards. It appeared to be a celebration of sorts. The men smiled approvingly at Rose, still an attractive woman in her mid-forties, and looked favorably at Zdenka, an attractive, mature-looking sixteen-year-old. Jaroslav was awestruck by so many uniforms and guns. The border guards didn't see many newcomers in the area, especially attractive women from Prague. Rose and Zdenka became the center of attention.

One officer, who commanded the most respect, seemed suspicious. He was wondering what Rose was doing in this restricted region. He asked how she received permission. "Dear lady, I don't wish to sound presumptuous, but what are you and your children doing here? This is a restricted area. How did you come here without special permission?"

"I have a letter of access from the Ministry of Interior," Rose replied in a nonchalant manner. "The healthy mountain air is necessary for my son's recovery. I'm sure the innkeeper also has a copy."

He nodded approvingly and said, "Yes, this area is well-known for the therapeutic mountain air. Long walks in the woods will help your son recover quickly." He also knew that to question the decisions from the Ministry of Interior might mean the end of his position or the prospect of any future promotions.

During their staple meal of dumplings, pork, and sauerkraut, Rose asked the officer, "Why are you celebrating?"

"We are all going home soon," he explained in a beer-relaxed mood. "Our government, in their infinite wisdom, cowed by the Russians, is replacing all Czech border guards with Russians from their eastern provinces. They blame us Czechs for allowing too many of our countrymen to escape," he said. "The Russians don't trust us."

Rose and Zdenka did their best to hide their fear. Jaroslav cheerfully piped in, "We are going to look for deer."

The officer smiled. "There are plenty of deer but also elk, wolves, and some black bears." He looked at Rose and said, "May I suggest that you stay on marked trails. There may be some buried land mines left over from the war. We cleared many out over the past four years, but just last month, one of my men carelessly stepped on one close to the border and blew his leg off." *That will scare them*, he thought, knowing well that there were no mines in the area.

Rose played the game and replied, "I assure you we will not venture into any restricted areas, but thank you for the advice." She remembered reading an article some months ago in a Prague newspaper that all the land mines along the borders were cleaned out. She knew he was trying to scare them.

The innkeeper approached their table and asked, "Please accept my apology for this interruption, but may I speak with you privately in the next room, Mrs. Kozak?"

"Yes," Rose replied, her curiosity piqued. She excused herself and joined him at a table in the next room.

"Are you and your children enjoying the food?" he asked obsequiously.

"Are your accommodations satisfactory, and is our fresh country air helping your son?"

Rose wondered what he was getting at. He sounded so fawning. His clumsy effort at small talk began to worry her. She answered with a smile,

"Everything is fine. Thank you for your concern. What was it you wanted to ask me?"

With an uneasy look on his face, he leaned closer and whispered, "I was born in Modrava, the nearby village, and know the countryside well. I know the mountains, every path in the forest, and roads on both sides of the border."

What he just said unsettled her. She quickly interrupted him and asked, "Why are you telling me this?"

He leaned closer and said, "I guided many people across the border and have relatives on the German side, which helped them."

Rose sensed he was attempting to expose her and acted baffled. "What are you trying to say?" she asked.

He noticed her anxiety but continued, "I need a pickup truck but don't have the money." Then he startled her by looking directly into her eyes and asked, "Do you know of anyone who may need my services?"

"Of course not," Rose replied. "I have no intentions of leaving Czechoslovakia illegally and don't know anyone who would. I am an American citizen and am waiting to immigrate to the United States with my family as soon as my husband returns from Switzerland and finishes his work in Prague. I will not leave this country illegally and endanger my children. Our emigration is pending, and as soon as my husband returns from Switzerland, our papers will be approved by the Ministry of Interior. My homeland is the United States of America, where I hope to take my family." She took a deep breath, raised her voice, and asked angrily, "Are you implying that I wish to cross the border illegally!?"

"No, please, don't take offense," he stammered, caught by surprise.

Rose felt she had gained ground and pushed the issue. "Why are you pestering me like this? Perhaps I should report your accusations to Mr. Slepak at the Ministry of Interior, who gave us permission to travel here."

"I beg your pardon, madam. Please forget what I said. I hope all turns out well for you and your family." He stood up and hurriedly walked out of the room without asking any more questions.

Rose pondered the meeting, confounded by what consequences it may bring. Her anxiety disappeared the next day when, to her surprise, she noticed a distinct graciousness from the officers and other soldiers towards her and her family, as if she exonerated herself from some sort of treachery.

Chapter 15

Eternal vigilance is the price
of liberty.

--Thomas Jefferson

Rose hoped for a successful meeting with the guide. She was certain he knew the area well and would know how to get them across the border safely. But was he honest?

Zdenka noticed a young border guard glancing her way during supper. She mentioned to Rose that it might be a good idea if she returned his attention to see if he had any additional information that may prove useful to them. Rose said, "By all means, smile at him."

She returned his smile and, once they had completed their meal, he came over and introduced himself. "Please forgive my forwardness, but we do not see many young ladies in this area. My name is Pavel. I have lived in the barracks above the inn for six months now and look forward to returning to Prague in the next few days. However, I was wondering if, in the meantime, I may be of any assistance? I know the area well and would be happy to show you our countryside."

Rose realized that his offer may be helpful and said, "Thank you for such a kind offer, but we are to meet a local guide tomorrow morning, who promised to help us find deer. If he doesn't show up, we would be happy to have you join us. "

"I have tomorrow afternoon off and will stop at the inn to see if you are still here." He was dumbstruck at the prospect of getting to know Zdenka and stammered, "I hope your guide doesn't show up."

That night, Rose and Zdenka slept little, knowing time was running out. With Russian troops arriving any day, they laid their hopes on the guide they were to meet the next morning.

Jaroslav was the first up the next morning, excited about the prospect of looking for deer. Rose asked him to calm down because the guide wasn't coming until 10:00 AM and she had to speak with him first before they went anywhere. Jaroslav was too excited to just sit around. After eating a breakfast of dark bread, a hunk of cheese, and fresh milk from nearby cows, he took the dog to the river and skipped flat stones across the water.

Meanwhile, Rose and Zdenka waited in the dining room, drinking coffee, too nervous to eat. They pretended to read a two-day-old newspaper from Prague but kept an eye on the wall clock. The innkeeper's wife, sensing their anxiety, came over with a fresh pot of coffee and asked, "Is there anything I can help you with?"

"We are planning to start on our daily hike," Rose said, keeping calm, "and are waiting for a guide, who will show us where the deer are."

"All local guides are lazy," replied the innkeeper's wife, with a wave of her hand. "Why would anyone hire a guide just to look at deer instead of hunting them? They eat until their stomachs burst, drink all night, and sleep all day. They are good for nothing!"

Rose laughed and explained, "This is a special treat for my son. He has never seen a deer before." Her curiosity satisfied, the woman walked away, muttering about the waste of money. Ten o'clock came and went without the guide showing up. They waited until eleven thirty.

Rose admitted to herself that the one hundred dollars she gave the guide was lost. She knew their chances of escaping were diminishing. Zdenka, sensing her mother's despair, said, "Maybe he has his days mixed up. He may still show up." Rose knew Zdenka was trying to cheer her up and decided to not allow despair to dominate her. She stood up briskly, surprising Zdenka, and walked towards the front door. "Where are you going?" Zdenka asked, perplexed, standing up and running after her.

"Come," she told Zdenka, "we need exercise to clear our thinking." She did not have a definite plan but knew that walking made her feel better.

"Why don't we walk to the village, to the guide's house? I remember where it is," Zdenka suggested.

"Excellent idea!" replied Rose. She yelled at Jaroslav, "Don't go anywhere. We will be back in a little while."

"Don't worry; I'll stay here," replied Jaroslav, preoccupied with skipping stones, not worried about their problems.

They walked decisively to the village. Zdenka led the way, remembering where the guide lived. She wrapped a scarf over her head so she would not be recognized by anyone from her summer trip to the area. The village looked desolate in the gray October day. They noticed several elderly women wearing babushkas on their heads, carrying firewood on their backs, and hurrying to their homes, afraid of something. It seemed so strange, Zdenka thought, compared to the way she remembered it just a few months ago. They walked up to the house with the thatched roof and knocked on the door. There was no answer.

After several knocks, Rose decided to look for answers at the nearby courthouse. They walked through the door and were met by a heavy-set man in a rumpled, gray suit, who asked, "How may I help you? We don't have many visitors in this area anymore."

"Why is that?" Rose asked, attempting to look clueless, in an effort to quell any suspicions. "This is a beautiful area. Why does your town look so desolate?"

"Well," he said, feeling grateful to be able to show off his knowledge, "once the area became restricted to tourists, many of the guides and small shop owners lost their source of income. They were forced to work in the state-owned factories or on the collective farms to support their families."

"Did you know the person living in that house with the thatched roof?" Rose asked, pointing to it through the window.

He looked at her suspiciously and replied, "He was a woodcutter who was arrested by the authorities for trying to bribe border guards with American dollars. Why do you ask about him? Did you know him?"

"No, I did not!" Rose replied, frightened by what she just heard. "I was told he was an experienced guide, but knew nothing about him."

"Why would you be inquiring about a guide? What are you doing in this restricted border area?" he persisted.

By now, Rose knew he was suspicious and immediately took the offensive. "My children and I received permission from the Ministry of Interior to vacation here for therapeutic reasons. I asked about someone to guide us around the area and was told that the man who lived in the thatched-roof house was a guide. You are welcome to call the Ministry of Interior in Prague and question their reasons." That did it. He did not want anything to do with the dreaded Ministry of Interior and wished her well. She grabbed Zdenka's hand, and they hurried back to the inn.

Chapter 16

I expect the best and with God's
help will attain the best.

--Norman Vincent Peale

The young border guard they met the night before approached them with a bright smile and said, "Hello. What a beautiful afternoon." It was 1:00 PM, and they had just returned to the inn.

His exuberant greeting caught Rose off balance.

"I hope your guide didn't show up so that I may offer you my services. I know the countryside well and would very much enjoy showing you around."

"That would be wonderful. It is so kind of you to offer," Rose replied without a second thought, knowing the possibilities. Zdenka read her mother's mind and gave him a friendly smile.

They yelled after Jaroslav, asked the innkeeper's wife to pack several sandwiches and two flasks of water, and then set off on a midday hike. Rose and Zdenka, being of the same mindset, had many questions for the young border guard. The guard, Pavel, happy at the prospect of getting to know Zdenka, was only too happy to help. During their hike into the hills, Rose asked Pavel, "Are there still any hidden land mines from the war in this area?"

"There may still be a few that were missed, Mrs. Kozak, but most were dug up soon after the war," Pavel answered.

"Would there be any along the firebreaks?" Zdenka asked

"The firebreaks are in a high-visibility area and they would be the first and easiest to be cleared of mines," He said. "There are tall forest ranger towers every few miles along these firebreaks, so if any mines ever exploded, they would be noticed and the area would be immediately inspected and cleared by the border guards. I think our commander likes to scare people into believing that there are mines out there to keep them from escaping. As long as I have been here, I never heard of any mines exploding in this area."

"Does this mean that you must sit in the observation tower and scan the countryside for hours on end? Doesn't that get boring?" asked Rose jokingly.

"Most of the towers are old and rickety, but every once in a while, when there isn't much work to do, our commander makes us climb up some of the sturdier ones and scan the countryside with binoculars," Pavel replied, full of self importance, happy to show Zdenka how smart he was. He continued with a sheepish grin, "The work is very boring, so we usually sneak up good Czech beer."

As they hiked along the hillside, Pavel pointed west and said, "The German border is a mere fifteen miles from where we are standing." Zdenka noticed they were close to the familiar Station of the Cross. They could see the ranger tower across the valley.

She asked Pavel, "Do the firebreaks cross into Germany?"

"Yes, many firebreaks cross the borders into Germany and Austria," replied the clueless young border guard. "There is a decades-old reciprocity between both countries, dating back to the Hapsburgs, in an effort to prevent forest fires from spreading. Some firebreaks are fifty to seventy kilometers long and cross the border in many places." He was happy to be noticed by Zdenka.

"Is there anyone in the tower across the valley?" Rose asked, pointing to the tower.

"No, that one is in bad shape," replied Pavel. "It has planks missing on the observation platform. Just last week, one of my comrades almost fell through the rotten wood while standing up there, observing the countryside. It is now deemed unsafe and marked for demolition. It will probably collapse in a good storm unless the Russians decide to rebuild it."

"Why would the Russians want to rebuild it?" Rose asked, very interested, contemplating the specter of Russian troops on the Czech border.

"The Russians are paranoid of the West. I was told that sometime soon they plan to totally secure the borders by building cement bunkers and laying barbed wire and mines along it."

Rose, by now, had heard enough and was anxious to return. She said, "Pavel, we are tired of walking so far and don't want Jaroslav to wear himself out. Let's turn around."

Evening shadows stretched across the valleys. They still had another hour of hiking before they reached the inn.

Once again, they returned during supper. The dining area was full of celebrating soldiers, all anxious to go home the next day. The smell of sauerkraut, pork, and beer permeated the smoke-filled room. Rose listened closely to their banter and heard they were ordered to evacuate the barracks by noon the next day. The Russians were expected before 6:00 PM the following evening.

During dinner, Pavel asked Rose, "Mrs. Kozak, may I call on your daughter Zdenka when you return to Prague?"

"Yes, that would be fine, Pavel, but we do not plan to return for at least another week," replied Rose, smiling knowingly at Zdenka. She knew there would be no return. *Maybe someday*, she thought. Pavel was overjoyed at the prospect of meeting up with Zdenka in Prague. He wished them all good night, stating that he had to finish packing for his early departure home. He winked at Zdenka and left.

Rose understood the young man's desire to return home. She guessed his age to be about twenty and would not think less of him for being homesick. She remembered that it had been eighteen years since she saw her parents' faces. The lingering pain of homesickness was still there, deep inside. She momentarily languished in the bittersweet emotion of remembrance. What was her sister Josephine's life like, being married to a doctor with a budding family? What was Annie, her youngest sister, who just turned thirteen, doing? She was in the eighth grade by now, living in Highland Park, Michigan, with her parents. Did she have a boyfriend? She thought about her brother Jim, recently married, a young executive with Socony Vacuum Co. What was his wife like? she mused. Did they have any children? Would she ever see them all again? All these thoughts raced through her mind as she recalled segments of her mother's letter that she received over a year ago. She quickly dismissed those emotional thoughts, knowing her children and their escape must come first, before those questions would be answered.

One last thought entered her mind. *What will Anthony think if I fail to bring our children safely out of Czechoslovakia?* This played on her mind. She remembered how she lost that diamond necklace before the war and all the times she deceived him. *Will he ever forgive me if I fail?* she wondered.

She hoped Pavel's information was correct. The evening faded into a night of foreboding as the Kozaks returned to their room. Rose and Zdenka had much to discuss and think about. Jaroslav was tired and fell asleep immediately. Rose and Zdenka quietly made plans. They knew the next day would be difficult.

Chapter 17

Get action. Seize the moment.
Man was never intended to be
an oyster.

--Theodore Roosevelt

Jaroslav awoke to the gentle touch of his mother's hand. "Wake up," she whispered. It was dark, and he instinctively felt alert. This was the earliest they had ever gotten up. There was an air of tension in the dimly lit room. Rose and Zdenka were packing their rucksacks, moving quietly around the room. Rose carefully packed the framed picture of Michael the Archangel guarding two children walking near a stream. *Please guide us safely,* she thought to herself.

Rose, noticed Jaroslav's anxiety. She quietly explained, "We need to get up early to look for deer because they graze for their breakfast very early."

The explanation sounded reasonable to Jaroslav, and it fueled his impatience to get started. He quickly dressed and asked his mother, "Can I take the dog with us?"

"No, the dog would scare the deer away," she replied, hoping it would satisfy his curiosity. They quietly stepped out of their room and walked down the dimly lit hall to the stairs. The inn was old, and the stairs creaked as they slowly walked down to the main floor and out the door, into the darkness of the early morning. Zdenka momentarily slipped into the pantry before running out after Rose and her brother. It was 5:00 AM, October 12th, 1949. No one noticed them leave. They crossed the river next to the inn and hiked in the direction of the mountain path, along which stood the Stations of the Cross. Their breath was visible in the cold, crisp air as they hurried across an open field to the security of the fir trees marking the base of the hill where their familiar path began.

Rose felt safer in the woods but knew she would be questioned if they were caught this early in the morning by a returning border patrol. Although they were not in a restricted area, they would still raise suspicion. She said to Zdenka, "Listen for any unusual noises," and to Jaroslav, "Walk quietly so you do not scare any deer." *So far, so good*, she thought, knowing it was just the beginning. Light from the eastern sky slowly penetrated the dissipating clouds as they hiked up the serpentine path. Rose, ever watchful, hurried them along. She wanted to reach the familiar Station of the Cross before 8:00 AM. It was a schedule she kept in the back of her mind, knowing they had to cover a great distance before the end of the day. She only hoped Jaroslav was well enough to keep up the pace. As they hiked ever higher up the path, sunshine crested over nearby hills and cast light across the deep valleys below. It promised to be a warm day. They hiked at a steady pace now, continually ascending the side of this small mountain looking for the beginning of the Stations of the Cross. This was near the area of Cerna Hora on the Czech side and Grosse Rache on the German side of the border. The small mountains averaged between 1,300 to 1,500 feet—larger than hills but smaller than the Tatras of northeastern Slovakia or the Alps of western Austria. Nevertheless, with their fast pace, it was a tedious climb for the Kozak family. Jaroslav, running ahead, was first to spot the beginning of the Stations of the Cross. "I found it," he yelled, pointing up the trail. Here, the grade became steeper, with an ever-deepening valley below. *Good*, thought Rose. They were getting closer to their familiar spot. She only wished Jaroslav wouldn't run so much, hoping he would save his energy for the day ahead.

She wondered how long she could fool him with her deer story. She didn't have to worry. Zdenka played her part well by periodically pointing up the trail or into the valley claiming, "Look there's a deer." Jaroslav's enthusiasm seemed never-ending; he ran to and fro like a dog after a phantom rabbit. They hiked their way to the side of the mountain they knew well. There was the Station of the Cross so familiar to them. Across the valley, on the opposite slope, stood the ranger tower next to the firebreak that cut to the west. Rose took a deep breath and said a prayer. She knew this was the point of no return. Once they crossed the valley and climbed their way to the ranger tower, they were in a restricted area, clearly marked with bold signs in German: *Grenze-Verboten!* Every Czech knew what those words meant, and ignorance would not be acceptable to the authorities. Besides, Rose was tri-lingual, and should they be caught, the authorities in Prague would know that she understood the sign.

110

Rose hesitated, pulled a small notebook out of her bag, and, with a pencil, wrote the following: "On this day, October 12th, 1949, I, Rose Kozak, looking to the west from this Station of the Cross, made the decision to escape to freedom with my daughter and son. May God watch over us." She tore the paper out of her note pad, folded it up, and placed it into the wooden drawer below the carving of Christ carrying the cross.

"Let's go!" Rose said, grabbing Zdenka and Jaroslav. "We must run down this open hillside into the shadows of the valley below before anyone spots us." Jaroslav wasn't sure how this was connected to any deer sightings, but it seemed like a fun thing to do, so he ran as hard as he could. Rose and Zdenka tried to make a game out of it by pretending to chase him. They reached the bottom, out of breath, only to find they had to ford a whitewater stream about six feet wide. It seemed shallow, but the water was ice cold and the exposed rocks were moss-covered and slippery. Rose and Zdenka carefully stepped on the rocks near midstream and swung Jaroslav across. No one got wet, and Jaroslav thought it was exciting.

The valley was overcast with shadows. It was mid-morning, and the sun's rays barely flickered through the dense tree cover. The air was damp and smelled of rotting trees and mushrooms. It felt primeval, but it was safe. Rose didn't waste any time. After a few minutes rest, she got them up, saying, "Come, we cannot stay here all day," and herded them up the forested hill towards the ranger tower at the top. She knew they had many miles to go and not enough time. There were no paths, just wild forest. Up they hiked in what they thought was a straight line; however, as they neared the top, they realized that the tower was still about a quarter mile to the west. *It just seemed so much closer from the opposite side of the valley*, Rose thought. They reached the tower along the edge of the wide firebreak and decided to rest. Zdenka took out her little map and studied directions.

"If we follow this firebreak, it should lead to the border. It looks like the correct way," she concluded.

"As long as it progresses in a straight line, it will be easy to follow, but if it starts to curve on the other side of that hill," replied Rose, pointing across the valley, "we may need to change direction. Do you have your compass?"

"Yes, I do," Zdenka replied, pulling the compass out of her pocket. "I also have matches in a water-proof cylinder," she said, showing those as well.

"Good; they may come in handy later in the evening," Rose said, hoping they would be near the border by then.

They decided to follow the edge of the firebreak hidden by the forest, lessening their chances of being spotted. They noticed it descended down the other side, into a wide valley with a river running through it. There was a black paved road on the other side of the river. Rose knew they needed to ford the river and cross the road. They carefully started their descent, staying in the shadows of the fir trees that marked the edge of the firebreak. Jaroslav still wasn't sure what they were doing or where they were going, but he liked the stealth part and played along. As they neared the bottom, Rose noticed that the river was at least thirty feet wide and fast-flowing. The sun was bright, and there was no wind. Flies were lazily buzzing around them, bees were collecting pollen from the wildflowers, and the sound of crickets could be heard in the still October morning. It was quiet and peaceful by the water's edge. The river was shallow but cold. They took off their hiking boots and socks, listened for any strange noises, and then stepped into the icy water. Rose and Zdenka held Jaroslav's arms as they awkwardly walked through the knee-deep water. The blacktopped road on the other side was baked by the bright sun and felt good on their bare, icy feet. Jaroslav wanted to sit on the warm pavement to put his shoes and socks on, but Rose and Zdenka, aware of the danger, picked him up and pulled him into the forest on the other side. He started to feel irritated. He had had nothing to eat since he got up, and the constant hurrying and wading through icy water wore him out. Besides all that, he still hadn't seen the deer his mother promised him. His leg was hurting, and he started to whimper.

"I don't want to go any farther," he said. "I don't care about looking for deer. I just want to go back."

It must have been close to noon, and Rose decided he needed food. At that moment, they heard noise from motorcycles.

Rose yelled to Zdenka, "Quick, hide in that pit over there!" pointing to an uprooted tree. She grabbed Jaroslav, and with Zdenka's help, pulled him twenty feet into the crater of an old spruce, the victim of a severe storm.

An army convoy of trucks and motorcycles appeared on the nearby road, traveling fast, away from the border area. Jaroslav, feeling his mother's fear, squeezed between her and Zdenka. They were only thirty feet from the road, hidden behind the uprooted tree. From their vantage point, they could still see their wet footprints on the paved road. They held their breath as the motorized troops drove by. They were Czech border troops evacuating the border. They were driving too fast to notice the clearly visible footprints. Rose whispered a thankful prayer and knew they needed to eat something to keep up their strength. When the last of the convoy passed, she reached into her rucksack and pulled out two cans of sardines that she saved from one of Anthony's trips to Denmark. Zdenka, on the other hand, surprised the family with a loaf of dark bread she had taken from the inn's larder.

They rested against the side of the crater and ate their lunch. Feeling rejuvenated, they once again climbed up the hill, heading west. They kept to the side of the firebreak, following the sun's rays through the trees.

By now, Jaroslav was suspicious of this hike. He now knew they didn't wish to be seen by the border guards. The idea that they were doing something so secretive and adventurous invigorated him. With renewed energy, he happily trekked along between Zdenka and Rose.

They slowly hiked their way up anther hill. Zdenka checked her map and consulted with Rose, and both decided they were heading in the correct direction. As they reached the summit they noticed another empty ranger tower. When they were convinced there was no one around, Rose suggested to Zdenka, "Why don't you climb up and scan the countryside, just to make sure there isn't any danger ahead." Zdenka climbed to the top. It provided a vista of neighboring hills for perhaps six miles. She guessed they hiked about eight miles so far. Rose, checking her watch, noticed it was 3:00 PM and thought they probably had another four hours before their absence would raise suspicion at the inn. She hoped they would not be missed until much later.

From her vantage point, Zdenka could see another ranger tower on the far side of a neighboring mountain. Their firebreak led in that direction, following the path west in the afternoon sun. They rested briefly and hiked on, keeping to the side of the firebreak. Around 4:00 PM, as the sun weakened, Rose and Zdenka felt it was safe to walk in the center of the firebreak without having to tangle their way through the side underbrush and trees. By this time, afternoon shadows diffused visibility from afar. They also felt safe in the knowledge that it would be some time before the Russians secured the border from the departing Czechs.

Jaroslav's leg began to ache. He was used to long hikes, but this was definitely longer than any he had taken! "Mother," he cried, "my leg hurts and I am tired." Rose knew this would happen. She gave him an aspirin and an apple from her rucksack. They rested for a few minutes before resuming their hike. Rose consulted with Zdenka and both decided they may have to carry him if the pain increased. At this time, Rose sat down with Jaroslav and explained that they were escaping from the Communists into West Germany to reunite with his father.

"Jaro, you must be brave," she said. "Please understand that this is our only way out of Czechoslovakia. I tried many other ways, but they didn't work."

Hearing all this from his mother confirmed his thoughts that they were just trying to fool him with those deer stories. He felt more important than his six years and wished they had confided in him sooner. The aftermath of the war matured many young kids at that time. *She has confidence in me*, he thought, feeling better. If it meant meeting his father sooner, he was for it.

Once again, they continued their journey. They descended into another valley lush with evergreens. The changing colors of leaves on poplars and oaks and the light haze from the warm earth, in conflict with the approaching cool evening air, underscored the autumn afternoon.

Suddenly, Rose saw a reflection in the distance. Thinking it may be something metal, perhaps a gun or a helmet, she asked Zdenka, "Did you notice that flash of light over there in the valley?"

"It's the ebbing sun shimmering over water," replied Zdenka, pointing to a stream in the distance. With her keen eyesight, she was the first to see it on the far side of the valley they were descending. By now, they were all tired and dehydrated. The apples Rose packed for the trip helped, but nothing tasted as good or was as refreshing as water from a cold mountain stream. They hurried down to the inviting water and drank heartily, splashing water on their faces and necks. Rose took an extra undershirt out of her rucksack, soaked it in the cold water, took Jaroslav's jacket and shirt off, and wiped his upper body with it.

"Oh! That's cold!" he complained, shivering. He had to admit, however, that it certainly revived him. She used it as a cold compress around each of their necks. They all felt better.

The map of the escape.

Chapter 18

When every physical and mental resource
is focused, one's power to solve a problem
multiplies tremendously.

--Norman Vincent Peale

Dusk was approaching; the air turned noticeably cooler. Zdenka rubbed the numbness out of her hands before reaching into her pocket to pull out her map. She checked the map once more in the ebbing twilight and noticed the stream flowing west, paralleling their firebreak in a zigzag, meandering fashion. She knew the firebreak would soon become indistinct in the coming darkness and felt it would be easier to hike along the stream.

Zdenka carefully studied the map and said to Rose, "There is enough twilight left to follow the firebreak across one more hill. It will be faster than walking all the way around and should not take more than an hour. I'm confident we will pick up the stream on the other side."

As they reached the top of one more hill, Rose checked her watch in the fading light; it was now 8:30 PM.

"Zdenka," she whispered, "we don't have much time before we are missed at the inn. You know they will start looking for us."

"Yes, but we have hiked for over thirteen hours and have a good head start on anyone trying to follow us. The border should not be much farther."

The stream Zdenka hoped to follow was nowhere in sight. The terrain was leveling out. A light breeze blew through the pine trees, bending the tops with a soft swishing sound. Several deer rushed out of the bushes.

"What was that?" Jaroslav yelled, giving them all a good scare.

"Just deer," replied Rose, recovering first. Jaroslav was hanging on to Zdenka, frightened. The firebreak faded into darkness. There was no moon.

Zdenka, attempting to cheer up Rose, said, "A patrol will have a hard time finding us in this darkness."

"True," replied Rose, "but we don't want to lose our way west either."

"Maybe we should just stop here, spend the night, and continue at first light," suggested Zdenka, fearing the loss of direction in the approaching darkness.

"Not a good idea," replied Rose. "I fear the Russians are already looking for us." She heard that these particular Russian soldiers that were sent to guard the Czech-West German border came from the far eastern provinces and were known for their brutality. They were Asians who had nothing in common with people of Slavic origin, like the Czechs, and were told to show no mercy to anyone caught escaping. Rose shuddered at the prospect of being caught and the consequences to her family. Deportation for her and the adoption of her children by a Communist family were not options she would ever consider.

Rose peered into the shadows, pulling Jaroslav along, and asked Zdenka, "Are we walking in the right direction? It's becoming difficult to see anything."

Zdenka pulled the waterproof cylinder out of her jacket, struck a match, and held the flame up to her small compass. She cupped her hands to hide the light in the darkness, took a reading, and said, "Yes, we are still heading west but we must be careful to not walk in circles." The heat from the match warmed her cold hands, but she knew that light from a match on a dark night could be seen from a great distance by an alert border patrol. She blew the match out immediately.

The hard ground they walked on turned mossy and wet. The smell of rotting wood permeated the damp air. In their effort to find dry ground, they became disoriented in the moonless night.

They found themselves in a heavily wooded marshy forest. Gnarled old tree roots protruded through the spongy ground, slowing their progress. Noise from wild animals running through the darkness fueled their fear. They imagined that Russian patrols were looking for them by now. Elks were mating, fighting each other for their mate. Their rutting noises and the booming crashes of antlers among young bucks anxious to prove their supremacy over the herd echoed through the night. Jaroslav had reoccurring pain in his right hip after so much walking. He felt his mother's and sister's fear but was too tired to care. He stumbled along between them, holding on to their hands. As long as he held their hands, he felt safe.

Suddenly, Rose realized she was walking in ankle deep water. "I'm standing in water. Be careful where you step!" she yelled to Zdenka and Jaroslav, but it was too late. In their exhausted state, they didn't realize they had walked into a marsh. Thick muck stuck to their shoes, and a loud sucking sound was heard with each step.

"Help, I'm sinking!" shouted Zdenka. She was hanging on to Rose and Jaroslav, pulling them down as they all hung on to each other. Rose stood firm, leaned forward, and pulled Zdenka out of the sucking hole. She then picked up Jaroslav to keep his feet out of the water. He was heavy, and after a short distance, she was laboring under his weight.

Seeing how Rose was struggling, Zdenka took Jaroslav out of her arms, saying, "Let me try carrying him for a while." Their wet shoes and clothing added to their weight and discomfort. Zdenka's skirt was drenched up to her waist, Jaroslav's knickerbockers were wet, and Rose's woolen skirt was soaked through.

Zdenka set Jaroslav down and said to Rose, "Mother, please stop, don't take another step. I don't want you to fall into a sink hole. I think we are skirting the Bohemian watershed and must be near the German border, possibly the headwaters of the Vltava River."

She reasoned that since the water was getting deeper and the Vltava River flowed in a northeasterly direction, they were heading the wrong way.

"Let's hold hands tightly and very slowly walk to our left. I think the water is shallower there." She said to Rose, "Let me switch places with you," and took the lead, taking small, careful steps, thinking she would recover quicker in case the water deepened. Zdenka knew a watershed area had underground springs and deep sinkholes. Rose carefully stepped through the watery mush, holding on to Jaroslav in case he fell. Zdenka's intuition was correct. She moved carefully until she reached solid ground at the edge of the swamp. They reached dry ground safely.

An owl hooted nearby. Small rodents scampered for cover lest they be spotted by the keen-eyed predator. Zdenka, ever alert, whispered to Rose, "I see a hut in the distance, standing on what appears to be a stone bridge." Rose squinted but didn't see anything. She was forty-two years old and her eye sight was not as good as Zdenka's.

The forest was alive with noise from nocturnal creatures. The sound of barking foxes chasing rodents resounded in the darkness. The forest was thinning out in this area, and light from the moon pierced through the shadows illuminating their way.

"Even the moon is finally coming to help us," Rose whispered with renewed hope, relieved they were out of the swamp.

"I was taught in the Girl Scouts that pale skin shines in the moonlight. We should rub dirt on our faces," replied Zdenka.

They scooped up dirt and gingerly rubbed it on their cheeks and foreheads. Zdenka scouted a short distance ahead to make sure the hut she saw was empty. As she approached the stone hut, she noticed the open door and cautiously stepped in. It was empty and smelled of sweat, tobacco, and stale beer. When her eyes adjusted to the darkness, she saw several empty mattresses lying on the floor, empty beer bottles, and a metal ashtray overfilled with cigarette butts, suggesting a hasty departure.

She returned quickly, telling Rose, "It must be a border guard hut. I noticed empty beds through an opened door and a strong smell of tobacco and beer. They must have been Czech border guards who received news that they were being replaced by Russians."

Since no one was around, they boldly stepped up to the hut and crossed the stone bridge. Water trickled underneath. Zdenka surmised that the bridge crossed a portion of the watershed. They walked along a dirt path that merged into a wide, dry wagon trail. It led to a clearing with fallen trees and chopped logs lying around the ground.

Rose looked concerned and voiced her suspicions to Zdenka. "With all these fallen trees and logs lying around, woodcutters must be working here and may return early in the morning. We certainly don't want them to find us." She pointed in the direction of the visible wagon tracks and asked, "I wonder where that wide wagon trail leads to?"

"It probably links to a main road heading east, to haul the lumber out, most likely to Modrava," replied Zdenka.

"In that case," Rose countered, "trucks carrying soldiers also have access to this area."

"How would they know where we are?" asked Zdenka. "Nobody knows which direction we took, and the border area is vast. I think you're worrying needlessly. We need rest."

Rose knew they could not go on without rest.

"We'll stop here, between these two logs, for the night," Rose replied. "Jaroslav cannot go any farther, and I don't want to re-aggravate his healing hip." She checked her wristwatch in the bright moonlight. "It's 1:00 AM. We have walked for nearly eighteen hours and must be close to the border. By morning we should be safe in West Germany."

She opened her rucksack and took out a raincoat, apples, and a can of smoked bananas, another treat from one of Anthony's trips to Scandinavia. They sat on the raincoat and ate, savoring every morsel.

Rose said to Zdenka, "We must be up at the break of dawn before the woodcutters or a Russian patrol finds us." Jaroslav ate an apple and a smoked banana and then fell asleep … but not for long.

Chapter 19

Let me assert my firm belief
that the only thing we have to fear is fear itself.

--Franklin D. Roosevelt

"What's that?" asked Jaroslav, waking up suddenly. Rose sat up and looked at her watch. It was 2:00 AM and the wind was whistling through the trees, raining leaves upon their camp, but from the distance, a distinct noise from a barking dog and strange voices permeated the darkness, coming ever closer. His mother and sister pulled him into their arms and huddled close.

Rose placed her index finger to her lips. "Keep still," she whispered. Their fear was contagious, and he started to shiver.

Rose, catching her breath, explained in a halting voice, "If we are caught, a Communist family will probably adopt you both, but no matter what happens, I will return to find you." It was the most devastating news Jaroslav had heard in his young life.

"Please don't leave us, Mother," he whimpered.

Rose touched Zdenka's arm. "Promise me you will not leave Jaroslav if I am deported."

Zdenka was at a loss for words. To calm Rose, she replied, "Don't worry, Mother, we will always be together," and put a protective arm around Jaroslav, wishing she was stronger than she felt.

Rose knelt a few feet away with the picture of Michael the Archangel guiding two children near a stream, which she had purchased during her earlier pilgrimage to Bila Hora, and prayed. Zdenka and Jaroslav huddled together, resigned to whatever would follow. The barking became louder, and the voices from the approaching patrol sounded strange, not Czech.

Zdenka whispered to Rose, "They don't sound Slavic. They must be the Asian Russians we heard about."

"Maybe they sent a patrol to find us," whispered Rose, motioning to Zdenka to keep her voice down. "I'm sure the lodge-keeper reported us missing by nightfall. In either case, stay quiet!"

A large German shepherd loped along the logging trail, right towards them. Picking up their scent, he crashed through the thicket, leaped over the logs, and bounded up to Rose. She was kneeling in prayer, holding the picture of Michael the Archangel. "My God," she cried in alarm, raising her arm to protect herself.

In that instant, gunfire erupted through the night. Booming staccato sounds of small arms fire echoed through the trees. The dog sniffed Rose and ran off, following loud commands from the patrol leader. The Russian patrol changed direction, heading towards the gunfire.

The Kozaks remained undetected. Rose, Zdenka, and Jaroslav didn't move. They were afraid to breathe lest their breath give them away. After several minutes, Rose slowly stood up and listened to the noise in the distance, trying to determine how far away the patrol was before moving. Satisfied the patrol was gone and the gunfire in the distance was diminishing, she grabbed Zdenka and Jaroslav by their arms. "Let's go!" she said, pulling them blindly through the darkness. They stumbled over exposed tree roots. Branches whipped their faces, and thorny bushes caught their sleeves as they sought a place of refuge. They finally slowed, gasping for air. Rose and Zdenka took turns carrying and pulling Jaroslav along. His broken hip ached, his feet were wet, and his mind was numb. He stumbled and tripped over every stick and stone in his path. They paused every sixty paces or so and listened for any noise of pursuit. Not hearing anything, they finally collapsed in a bushy, secluded part of the forest. Feeling safer in the thick woods, they huddled together for warmth and fell into a fitful sleep.

Eleven armed Czechs also attempted their escape that same night, about one mile north of the Kozak's camp. Unfortunately, they ran into a Russian patrol. A gunfight ensued. Six were shot, but five managed to escape into West Germany. Noise from their encounter diverted the patrol looking for the Kozaks and saved them from capture.

In the meantime, after what seemed like only minutes to Jaroslav, Rose quietly awakened him and Zdenka. "Hurry." she said. "We must move now, before the patrol returns to look for us. I'm worried their dog may find our scent."

A slight graying in the eastern sky slowly revealed the coming dawn. Soon light penetrated the forest canopy, giving the Kozaks greater visibility. Rose gave both her children an apple, the last of the food. They rose from their shelter, stretched their sore limbs, and hurried on their way. The forest was thinning out where they walked. Rose stumbled over an old moss-covered stone and fell.

"What in the world was that!" she cried, standing up and brushing dirt off her skirt.

"I think it's a border stone," Zdenka replied, bending down and scraping moss off the rectangular stone.

It was an old Austria-Hungary border stone with Bohemian markings on one side and German on the other. The problem with the shape of the stone was that it didn't tell them which way they should go. There wasn't a visible line they could cross; the border ran in an irregular direction. Zdenka noticed a small clearing in the woods with a path on the other side. She motioned to Rose, "It runs west. We should take it."

"We cannot stay here much longer," Rose agreed. "Take Jaroslav's left arm. I'll grab the right, and we'll run to the cover of those trees on the other side."

They grabbed Jaroslav by each arm and ran across the small meadow. His shoes barely touched the ground as he was hefted along between his mother and sister. They reached the trees undetected, plopped Jaroslav down, and stopped to catch their breath. All was quiet and serene. Sunlight was slowly breaking through the puffy clouds in the eastern sky. A light breeze rustled trough the leaves. Rose had a feeling of peace, and with increasing confidence, she whispered to Zdenka, "I think we made it." Zdenka nodded in agreement. Even Jaroslav felt they were out of danger. The path was nearby. They followed it down the mountain. Birds were chirping in the trees. The clouds overhead finally blew open, and the sun burst through, warming their backs as they followed the path, always heading west. They were exhausted but felt cautiously optimistic. Rose was in the lead. Jaroslav was in the middle, with Zdenka directly behind them. Rose heard an unusual noise. She raised her hand and motioned them all to keep still.

"Move off the trail, behind those bushes," she said, pointing to a thick clump of evergreens. They quickly moved off the trail and squatted behind the bushes. Within minutes, they heard voices in the distance becoming louder as they neared. From their cover, they saw several armed men walking up the trail, single file, towards them, unaware of anyone around them.

Rose wondered if they had actually crossed the border. The men were still too far away to determine what language they spoke. Rose heard that even West German border guards returned refugees for bounty. Too many

Czechs were fleeing their homeland, and the Russians paid a reward for any Czechs who were caught attempting to escape. The West German economy was in shambles at war's end; people along the border resorted to any means for money.

Rose would not allow creeping despair to replace her hopefulness, and whispered to Zdenka, "Stay with Jaroslav." Then she stood up and boldly walked towards the men in her path. When they spotted her, they stopped dead in their tracks and unstrapped their rifles. They wondered if this woman was possessed or was part of some trap.

"Halt!" they commanded in German. Their leader nervously asked, looking over Rose's shoulder, "What are you doing in these woods, so close to the border? Don't you know that this is a restricted area?"

Rose walked up to the startled leader and, in clear English, said, "Good morning! I am an American visiting West Germany with my children; we were hiking in your beautiful forest, became lost, and wandered aimlessly in the woods. We are hungry and thirsty. Would you be so kind as to point us in the direction of the nearest village?"

They looked at her dumbfounded. Rose realized they didn't understand her and repeated everything in German. The man's mouth was agape, trying to digest what he just heard. He knew how English sounded and showed deference towards Rose. He noticed Zdenka and Jaroslav peeking out from behind the bushes, worried about their mother. A smile broke out on his face and, in German, he said, "*Ungemoglich*" (unbelievable).

He motioned to Zdenka and Jaroslav, "Come, come, we will not hurt you. You belong here with your brave mother." The other border guards lowered their guns, realizing there was no danger. They gave the Kozaks some of their hard-crusted dark bread and hot coffee out of their thermos. The leader pointed down the path and said in German, "The village is approximately one and half miles down this path. Go with God!"

They were German border guards on their way up to guard their frontier. They found it hard to believe that an English-speaking, middle-aged woman with a teenage daughter and an invalid six-year-old son hiked through the dangers of the Bohemian Forest, evaded a Russian patrol, and escaped safely into West Germany.

The time was approximately 7:00 AM, October 13th, 1949. Rose noticed her watch had stopped at 2AM, the time they were almost captured; it was an auspicious moment, never to be forgotten.

Chapter 20

Only our individual faith in freedom
can keep us free.

--Dwight D. Eisenhower

Exhilarated by their successful escape, the Kozaks continued downhill, towards the village. In the distance, Rose heard singing in English. *How strange*, she thought. Through the trees, they noticed a clearing in the woods, where a kindergarten class was singing American nursery rhymes with their teacher. As the Kozaks approached, the children paused in their singing and looked at them, bewildered.

Rose knew they looked a sorry sight but walked up to the teacher anyhow and asked, out of curiosity, "Are you an American? You sound so fluent in English."

"Yes," the young lady replied with a smile. "I was born in Davenport, Iowa. My husband is a first lieutenant stationed in Straubing here in West Germany. I'm teaching German children English." But looking at the Kozaks in their dirty, exhausted state, she asked, "Where in the world did you come from? What happened to you, and where did you learn English?!"

"I was born in Dayton, Ohio," Rose replied, believing it was true. "We escaped from Communist Czechoslovakia, walked eighteen hours through the Bohemian Forest, were almost caught by a Russian patrol, and made it to the safety of West Germany."

The young teacher shook her head in disbelief. *A mother, a teenage daughter, and a young son, escaping across the border without help,* she thought. *Why that's unbelievable!* "Congratulations on your successful escape! The village is only another twenty-minute walk. Just stay on this path and it will lead you there. The people are very friendly but only speak German."

"That's okay," replied Rose. "My daughter and I both speak German."

Rose thanked her, and the Kozaks went on their way. As they neared the village, fatigue was finally taking its toll. They were dragging their feet as they passed by a small cottage on their way to the village. Smoke drifted out of the brick chimney.

An elderly, heavyset German woman was sweeping dirt out of the open doorway. She waved at them. "Come in, come in," she said joyfully in German. "There is plenty of food." Noticing their damp clothes, she continued, "Sit by the warm fire, where you can dry out your clothes," pointing to the hearth. The smell of potato-mushroom soup wafted across their nostrils, whetting their appetite. They hadn't eaten a complete meal in over twenty hours. The Kozaks carefully walked into the cottage with obvious hunger in their eyes but fully aware they were strangers in a foreign land. The woman, noticing their timidity, said in a friendly voice, "I have delicious hot soup and hard-crusted bread with butter. You look like you walked a great distance and must be hungry. Come in, eat, and rest. You are safe here."

"Thank you," replied Rose in German, accepting her offer, grateful for her generosity. Jaroslav was on his third bowl of soup when he noticed his mother becoming uneasy.

"Did you escape from Czechoslovakia?" the woman asked curiously.

"Yes," replied Rose, wondering why she asked. She obviously heard Jaroslav and Zdenka speaking in Czech and noticed their damp clothes. Rose knew they needed food and was willing to take the risk.

"How long were you walking?"

"Over eighteen hours," replied Rose.

The woman fiddled with her apron and frequently peered out her window, all the while saying, "Eat, relax, and let your clothes dry. After all that walking, you must be exhausted."

To Rose, her gestures and smile seemed insincere. *Something is wrong,* she thought.

Rose stood up, complimenting her for her generosity. She said in German, "My dear lady, thank you very much for your hospitality. Your food was delicious. Our clothes are dry and we are well rested but now we must be on our way." She noticed the grandfather clock on the wall chime 10:00 AM.

The big woman became less jovial and, in a constrained voice but still attempting to smile, said, "Please, you must stay a little while longer. My husband will be here shortly and, with his horse and wagon, will take your family to the American Army base."

Alarms went off in Rose's head. She had heard stories of German border people turning refugees over to the Communists for bounty. She quickly opened the heavy wooden door and urged Jaroslav and Zdenka out. "Run! We must leave now. Move!" They both jumped up and ran out the door.

The big woman tried to block their way, protesting loudly. Rose pushed her over a stool and followed her kids out the door, leaving the disheveled woman waving and yelling German expletives in the doorway.

They hurried towards the center of the village, looking for the police station or any presence of an American army base, where they would be safe. A cursory scan of the village revealed a village square with a fountain in the middle, several stores, a butcher shop, a grocery store, clothing and hardware stores, and a few women with babushkas wrapped around their heads, in long woolen skirts, carrying hand baskets, scurrying about. They looked at the Kozaks with suspicion, weary of strangers. Across the top of a large wooden door, on what looked to be a courthouse was the word "Zwiezel." Zdenka surmised that Zwiezel was the name of the town. Rose noticed a Jeep parked in front of a beer garden. Upon closer inspection, she noticed the white star on the door and the "U.S. Army" markings.

"Climb into that Jeep and stay there until I come out," she told Zdenka and Jaroslav. She entered the beer garden. A few minutes later, she came out with a befuddled sergeant and two U.S. soldiers.

They looked in amazement at Zdenka and Jaroslav sitting half asleep in the Jeep. "This is unbelievable," the sergeant said. "A mother and her two kids escaping through the Bohemian Forest into West Germany without any help." The other two soldiers nodded in agreement. By then, Zdenka and Jaroslav were fully awake and climbed into the back seat with their mother. Rose finally felt secure, sitting in an army Jeep protected by American soldiers. She contentedly listened and laughed at their banter. It felt good to be in the company of these funny, self-confident young men smoking their Lucky Strike cigarettes, showing off their wit to her and Zdenka. They each received Hershey chocolate bars and were driven to a U.S. army base near the town of Straubing, about a half-hour away.

Rose was questioned by the army staff while Jaroslav and Zdenka slept in their chairs in the reception room. A kind U.S. Army captain asked her a multitude of questions while his secretary typed all of Rose's answers. When Rose finished with the interrogation, she returned to the reception room and waited with her sleeping children for further processing.

Two military policemen entered with a very excited middle-aged man between them, happily exclaiming, "I made it. By God, I escaped!" Noticing the two sleeping children, he quieted down. The military policemen asked him to take a seat while they decided what to do with him. He sat near Rose and, nodding at Jaroslav and Zdenka, said, "Isn't it wonderful how easily they sleep?"

Rose noticed his mud-spattered overcoat with visible pajama pants and mud-caked slippers. She regarded him with suspicion. In a clipped voice, she said, "They earned the right to sleep, having hiked eighteen miles through the wilds of the Bohemian Forest. Why, what did you do?" she asked, irritated that he may wake her children. She also heard stories of Communist agents infiltrating U.S. army barracks located near the Czech border, to obtain information on families of refugees left behind. They would hold these family members hostage until the refugee returned. Rose stayed alert.

He noticed her ire and apologized, stating, "I also escaped from Czechoslovakia but on a motorcycle. I rode for hours in the dark before bursting across the border between two lumber trucks, fooling the unsuspecting border guards." He said, "I was a director in the Skoda Auto Factory in Plzen. The Communists came to my office and told me to declare my allegiance to the Communist Party and set an example to the management and workers in the factory. I told them that I thought there was going to be a vote, that I needed a couple of days to prepare my speech. They said I had one day to prepare but must have noticed my reluctance. The secret police came to my house in the middle of the night. It was about 1:00 AM when my wife and I awakened to a loud pounding on our front door. She jumped out of bed first, looked out the front window, and shouted, 'Get up and run. They have come for you!' She noticed three men by the front door and a fourth standing next to a black, four-door, Skoda-Tatra, the car most often used by the secret police. I leaped out of bed, stepped into my slippers, grabbed my overcoat out of the hall closet, and ran out the back door, down the alley, where I hid my motorcycle. I drove for hours in the dark, without my headlight, to the West German border. Once nearby, I hid in the bushes, waiting for an opportunity to shoot across. It was heavily guarded, but, after an hour or so, two lumber trucks approached the checkpoint. There seemed to be a problem with one of them, and as they waved the other truck past, I saw my opportunity and drove my motorcycle through the narrow opening between them, to freedom. My wife and I knew we lived on borrowed time, but until they trained someone to take my place, I felt safe. How stupid was I?!" he lamented. In a sad voice, he looked at Rose and continued, "You escaped with your children, but I left a wife and two teenagers behind. How will I go on without them?"

Rose, attempting to console the depressed man, said, "Others have done it; one of them was my husband. Faith will pull you through. Don't ever give up."

A short time later, a small bus drove the Kozaks to a heavily secured OSS (Office of Strategic Services) farm house near the base. The OSS was the predecessor to the CIA. They were given comfortable living quarters, plenty of wholesome food, and much-needed rest. They each took a bath and were allowed to sleep for at least ten hours. They were given clean clothes while their clothes were washed. The next day, a plain-clothed officer in the OSS said to Rose, "You and your children will undergo vigorous questioning, but we promise to make you as comfortable as possible." Rose was questioned intensely about the state of affairs in Prague, about the border guard station near their inn, about when the Russians replaced the Czech border guards, and how many she thought there were. They questioned Zdenka about Pavel's feelings towards being replaced by Russians. They studied her small map and asked her to draw the approximate location of the ranger lookout towers, how many she thought they saw along their journey, etc. They were mostly interested in Rose's account of the firefight the night of their escape. Even Jaroslav was asked about his experience in kindergarten and the Russian war films he was asked to watch. The questioning was intense but very friendly. Whenever they looked tired, the interrogators stopped. The questions resumed only after they were rested and fed.

Chapter 21

One joy dispels a hundred cares.

--Confucius

A week later, they were driven to a refugee camp located in the city of Munich, administered by the U.S. Army. Rose and her children were asked to stay there while their documents were processed and their escape documented for their eventual passports to Switzerland. Rose received permission to call Anthony in Basel.

Anthony answered on the third ring. "Hello," he said.

A pause followed, and then he heard Rose's unbelievable words: "My darling, we got out!"

He was overjoyed to hear her voice but, not knowing that they were forced to escape, asked, "Why didn't you take the train directly to Basel? As an America citizen, they would have let you."

Rose answered in a halting voice, "The Communists would not allow me to leave with Zdenka and Jaroslav. They gave me permission to leave, but not with our children. We escaped across the border by hiking through the Bohemian Forest. We are all well, and I'll tell you the whole story when we're together again."

Anthony was dumbstruck; he could not believe what he just heard. *Did she not say that, as an American, she and the kids would be allowed to leave?* Nevertheless, he was overjoyed that they were well and looked forward to an early reunion.

The refugee camp was policed internally by refugees from Serbia and Croatia. Most had been there since the war, after escaping the Nazis, but were not comfortable with returning to Tito's Communist Yugoslavia. This didn't bother Rose. She understood Croatian, a Slavic language similar to Czech, and was able to communicate with most of them.

One day during dinner, Rose heard several men discussing their escape from Czechoslovakia into West Germany.

"When did this happen?" she asked.

"It happened during the night of October 12ᵗʰ," they replied.

Surprised, she said, "That was the same night we escaped," pointing to Zdenka and Jaroslav, sitting next to her.

"We crossed the border," Rose said, "from the area near the Czech village of Modrava. We hiked through the Bohemian Forest and crossed into West Germany the next morning, near the village of Zwiezel. During the night, we were almost caught by a Russian patrol, but to our good fortune, they were distracted by nearby gun fire. Was that you?" she asked.

"Yes, it must have been us," the man answered. "There were eleven of us, but after the fight, only five of us survived and escaped into West Germany a few miles north of Zwiezel. We met with American soldiers who were on maneuvers in the area and were transported to Regensburg. The Americans processed our papers there and sent us here to Munich to wait for our immigration to be approved to the United States and Canada."

"You helped us escape," Rose explained. "We are in your debt. I cannot thank you enough. It is hard to believe how your tragic journey helped us. "

They exchanged names and names of relatives in the United States and promised to visit if possible. Twelve years later, one of the men, Richard Novotny, visited with the Kozaks in Detroit on his way to an engineering job in Alberta, Canada. He was hoping to court Zdenka, but by that time, she was already married. However, he continued to correspond with Anthony for many years.

Rose was happy they were finally in a safe place, away from the specter of abduction. She felt secure in her belief that once her papers were processed, the family would be united with Anthony in Switzerland.

They lived and slept in a room with about twenty other refugee women, all waiting to be processed for journeys elsewhere. It was a melting pot of various nationalities, languages, and dialects; however, everyone seemed to get along. Families were allowed to stay together. Single women were housed apart from single men, but they all shared a common dining area. Rose, Zdenka, and Jaroslav were housed in the single women's quarters.

Zdenka slept in an upper bunk bed with squeaky springs, and whenever she moved much at night, the bed squeaked loudly and the elderly woman below, Mrs. Sarah Berkowitz, would jab up with a knitting needle and yell, "Lie still!"

One morning, Zdenka woke up late and went into the women's shower room alone. Shortly after, Rose and others heard Zdenka screaming, "Help! Let me go, you pig!" A large male janitor had assaulted her. He was trying to tear her robe off when she screamed.

Rose ran into the shower room, lunged at the big man, grabbed his beard, scratched his face, and kicked him in the groin with all her might. "You depraved pervert! Not with my daughter, you don't," she yelled. The other women all joined her, yelling, kicking, and hitting him. He ran out, screaming for help from the Serb security police. A few days later, Rose was asked to answer questions by the police in the administration building.

"You created an incident over a small matter," said the police chief. "Had you come to us, we would have handled this with less physical abuse to the janitor. Did you know he needed stitches on his face?"

"Good," replied Rose. "He deserved what he got. Why was he allowed into the women's washroom? Don't you have female janitors? What good would it have done to call your police? By then, my daughter might have been raped by that pervert!"

"You are exaggerating the incident Mrs. Kozak, but I will investigate this matter further," he said. "We treat people decently here. Try not to be a troublemaker."

Rose had a petition signed by all the ladies in her section requesting female janitors. The police chief did not look favorably on Rose's attempt to change his policy. He did not take criticism from a woman lightly.

The Kozaks' emigration papers seemed to take a long time to be processed. Rose felt sure it had something to do with her speaking up. She decided on another plan.

Rose knew that the U.S. army officers overseeing the camp generally arrived around 8:00 AM each day, stayed in their offices on the top floor of the camp's administration building, and left by 5:00 PM.

INTERNATIONAL REFUGEE ORGANIZATION
AREA No. 7, M U N I C H
Luitpold Kaserne

Date: **11.11.1949**

GOOD CONDUCT STATEMENT

KOZAK Ruzena
I certify that Mr.~~Neperial~~.....................................
7,8.1907   Kutina
born.........................Birth Place...................
Kutina   Jugoslavia
District .... Country ....
899162   IRO-Area7
D.P. Card No ....!!!!!!!! Issued ....

In Camp ...., is resident of this camp
24.X.1949   11.11.1949
from .... to .... Bl. ....

Room ....

According to the Police Records of this camp, she/~~she~~ has not
been arrested or imprisoned, and has not been ~~in~~ involved in
criminal activity during these period of residence in this
Static/camp- ~~Transient Center~~.

CHIEF of POLICE

IRO Area 7.
Luitpold Kaserne
Munich

MIHAILO J. POPOVIC
Police Chief

Rose felt vindicated, and female guards replaced male guards in the
women's sector as a result of Rose's efforts.

Rose prepared herself the following morning. She was up early and, with a hot cup of coffee in her hand, stood near the entrance of the administration building and engaged in a friendly conversation with a camp guard.

"How are you this morning?" she asked with a friendly smile.

"Fine, madam," he replied.

As the U.S. army cars pulled up, Rose dropped her cup of coffee on the guard's shoe, distracting him, and ran up to a colonel as he was climbing out of his car. She grabbed his arm and quickly said, "I'm an American citizen. My brother-in-law was a major in the U.S. Army. He served in Berlin in 1945. Our emigration papers are being needlessly held up by camp administrators. Can you help me? "

The colonel was amazed and, against the guard's protests, he invited Rose to his office, where he asked his staff to check her story. In a short while, information came from the U.S. Consul in Munich. Rose's brother-in-law was indeed a doctor and major in the U.S. Army during the war; however, Rose was *not* an American citizen. They double-checked the information with the U.S. Embassy in Bonn.

"Unfortunately, Mrs. Kozak," the colonel said, "according to the records passed on to me from the U.S. Embassy in Bonn, West Germany; you are not an American citizen."

"That's impossible," replied Rose. "I lived in the United States for seventeen years. My parents are U.S. citizens, and so am I!"

This information surprised the entire Kozak family, including Anthony, who was waiting for news of their departure for Switzerland. Rose thought she was a citizen. She was never aware that Hedwig, her mother, feeling homesick, decided to leave Dayton, Ohio, while pregnant with Rose, and traveled to Kutina, Yugoslavia. She gave birth to Rose in her parents' home (the Schmidts) and returned to Dayton three months later. Hedwig and James Kousak became naturalized American citizens in 1932, two years after Rose's marriage to Anthony in Bratislava, Czechoslovakia. These convoluted circumstances began when Rose left the United States before becoming a naturalized citizen.

The same situation happened to her sister Josephine. Hedwig gave birth to Josephine in her parents' home in Kutina with the help of a midwife. Months later, they traveled to the United States, denying both sisters U.S. citizenship through country of birth. When Josephine found this out years later, she implored her parents to become naturalized, stressing the importance of U.S. citizenship. They became citizens; however, it was too late to help Rose. Josephine, reaching the age of majority before her parents became citizens, was naturalized one year before her marriage to Dr. Paul Ivkovich, a U.S. citizen of Serbian parents.

This revelation astonished Rose. *What else could possibly happen?* she wondered. Her main concern now was how to unite the family.

"How does this disclosure affect us?" she asked the colonel.

"At this time, I am not certain," he replied. "I suggest you return to your room for the time being while we investigate your problem."

Chapter 22

Life is not dated merely by years
Events are sometimes the best calendars

--Benjamin Disraeli

Anthony sent telegrams and letters to all the relatives in the United States, telling them of Rose's escape. The U.S. Army camp overseers were suddenly inundated with letters supporting Rose. They received letters from Senator Vandenberg's office; the Chrysler Corporation, where Rose's father worked; the American Consulate in Switzerland; Mr. Rittman of *Transport Magazine*; and, most important, a copy of the Swiss transit visa sent to the Czech government months before, allowing Rose and her children passage to Switzerland, which the Communists had denied.

The U.S. Army colonel called Rose to his office and said, "Mrs. Kozak, the United States government understands your plight. We are issuing you and your children a Displaced Person document allowing you to join your husband in Switzerland." It was wonderful news to Rose.

The U.S. Army administrators did not wish to keep the Kozak family apart any longer. Within three days, they allowed Rose, Zdenka, and Jaroslav to take a train to join Anthony in Switzerland. Rose even received a tepid apology from the camp's Serbian police chief (he was happy to see her go). Just before Rose left the camp, the rules were changed so that only female janitors were allowed in the women's section. She felt vindicated! All the ladies in the women's wing wished Rose well and thanked her for her efforts on their behalf. Even Mrs. Berkowitz, the chubby little lady who poked the knitting needle through Zdenka's mattress, gave Zdenka a big hug and wished her well.

Anthony received a telegram from Rose informing him of their departure from Munich. He met the train in St. Gallen, near Lake Constance, close to the borders of Switzerland, Germany, and Austria. He saw them waving through the window as the train pulled up. Rose jumped out before the train came to a complete stop and threw her arms around him. After reuniting with Rose, Anthony boarded the train with a suitcase. He had gifts for everyone. Jaroslav received a woolen sweater, Zdenka a blue scarf, and Rose a white shawl. Everybody was happy. The train crossed deep valleys, over stone bridges, across wide rivers, through hilly forests, on to Basel, Switzerland, their new home.

The Kozak family was once again united and began their new life together in Switzerland. Anthony, upon news of their arrival, had rented an apartment on 22 Lachenweg (Laughing Way) in Riehen, a northern suburb of Basel.

The history of Basel preempted that of Prague. Prague was believed to have originated around 750 AD. Basel was a Roman fortification called Basilia in 374 AD. Later, during the middle ages, it became a center of religious upheaval and the birth of Protestantism, a situation somewhat similar to Prague during the days of Jan Huss.

Each morning, Anthony walked thirty minutes to a street car, which he took to downtown Basel. From the street car station, he walked another ten minutes to his work at *Transport Magazine*, located in a historical townhouse on Spalentorweg 9. He continued his journalistic work, writing and translating from the various languages he knew into German, the official language of Switzerland.

Rose was aware of the social etiquette and understood why her parents wanted her to learn European culture and customs. There was so much more finesse than there was in Detroit before she left. On the other hand, people became friends much faster in the United States. They trusted each other quicker and greeted each other by their first names. She remembered how long it took Anthony to establish a close relationship with people at Rittman Ltd. A good example was when Anthony met Mr. Willy Forster.

Mr. Willy Forster, the controller of the company, and Anthony became good friends. Their families visited each other many times. However, in spite of the fact that they were good friends, they always greeted each other in a formal manner, as was the custom. Anthony always greeted his friend Willy as Herr Forster, and Willy always greeted his friend Anthony as Herr Kozak. This formal relationship between two good friends continued for twenty-eight years, in the many letters they wrote to each other and the long-distance telephone calls they made to each other. In July of 1977, Anthony and Rose returned to Switzerland to visit with their friends. On July 23rd, they enjoyed a wonderful meal that Mrs. Forster cooked and drank their share of good wine. It was at this time that Mr. Forster said to Anthony, "We have been good friends for all these years. Would you object to calling me Willy?" Anthony was overcome with emotion. He knew it was a great honor to be allowed to address someone in Europe by their first name.

He replied, "Not unless you object to calling me Anthony." Now their friendship was sealed. They were buddies. They finally switched from the formal to the familiar, and it only took twenty-eight years. This was a friendship that started in 1949 in Basel, Switzerland, at Transport Magazine, Anthony's first employer in the non-Communist world.

Rose and Mrs. Forster followed suit. Since their husbands changed their greeting from the formal to the familiar, they did, too. Mrs. Forster asked Rose to call her Rutli. Rose and Rutli became closer friends.

Jaroslav's name was changed to Jon. He entered the second grade in December 1949, in the Niederholz Schule, a public school in Riehen. Each day, he walked two miles to school. In class, the children sat at their desks with their hands behind their backs. It was a rule that prevented fidgeting and forced kids to pay attention. When they were asked by the teacher to respond, they stood up straight, responded courteously, and sat back down, placing their hands behind their back.

Zdenka, who already spoke German, a mandatory requirement in all Czech schools during the Nazi era, entered her senior year of high school in Basel and did well. After graduation, he was accepted into the prestigious Basel Institute of Arts.

Each morning, Rose walked twenty minutes to the farmers market in Riehen and purchased food for their mid-day and evening meals. At that time, they did not have a refrigerator. Most housewives walked to the market each day to purchase fresh produce and to the butcher shop for fresh meat.

One day, Jon received a large package from his Aunt Josephine and Uncle Paul from Reed City, Michigan. He opened it with great curiosity and, to his surprise, unpacked a Cisco Kid cowboy hat and a two-gun black leather holster with two silver cap guns. Excited, he quickly strapped the holster and guns to his waist, put on his cowboy hat, loaded caps into his guns, and stepped outside to wreak havoc on the neighborhood. Within a half hour, he had frightened the daylights out of at least four housewives by shooting his cap guns at them while they were sweeping their front steps. The cap guns made such a racket that the poor women thought they were actually being shot at and called the police.

Jon's adventure came to an abrupt end when the police car pulled up next to him as he was busily shooting everything in sight. They confiscated his guns and drove him home. Two officers, with Jon between them, walked into Rose's kitchen as she was preparing dinner. "Mrs. Kozak," said one of the officers, "we caught your son shooting his cap pistols at people in the street, frightening them. It is unlawful for children to play with guns in Switzerland. You and your husband will be charged in court for your son's misconduct."

"But they are harmless cap guns," she replied, bewildered.

"That doesn't matter," the police officer remarked. "We are a pacifist nation, and guns of any type are not allowed in our society. Please inform your husband that he will be required to appear in court."

Flabbergasted, Rose called Anthony at work to explain what seemed to her to be a silly situation. He wasn't pleased and said, "How could you allow Jon to walk out of our home with cap guns strapped to his waist? Didn't you know that toy guns are not sold anywhere in Switzerland? We are guests in this country under a temporary displaced person status. Our conduct is watched."

"Please don't be angry with me," replied Rose. "Boys played with toy guns in Czechoslovakia and Germany. All their heroes were soldiers. I did not know that something so trivial wasn't allowed in Switzerland."

Anthony hoped this incident would not impinge on their ability to stay and was not looking forward to his court date.

The judge, a man in his late sixties with a shock of thick, white hair and introspective blue eyes, looked down at Anthony from his bench and said, "Mr. Kozak, we take our laws of neutrality and pacifism very seriously. In this country, we hold the parents responsible for the acts of their children until age eighteen. You will be required to pay two hundred francs or spend three days in jail. I must warn you that jail time will reflect negatively on your displaced person status and may result in your deportation back to Czechoslovakia. Guns of any type reflect a propensity towards violence, especially in the hands of children. In our country, only soldiers and policemen are allowed to carry them. Please obey our laws if you wish to stay here!"

Anthony apologized to the judge and paid the fine, knowing any explanation would be futile. He knew Swiss laws were tough but fair and respected them for that.

The whole incident troubled Rose. She felt responsible and needed to clear her mind. She packed her rucksack and hiked the Jura Mountains for three days, sleeping in youth hostels. Zdenka cooked for Jon and Anthony during her absence. Rose returned tired but content, realizing that she only felt sorry for herself and that the judge was right. She should not have allowed Jon to walk outside with the cap guns and forgave Anthony for his anger. Hiking alone in the woods always revitalized her. Once again, there was peace in the family.

On some weekends, they traveled by train or bus to the Alps, where they spent the day hiking in the fresh air and looking for edelweiss, a pretty alpine flower with small, white buds and leaves with the texture of velvet. Closer to home, usually on a Sunday, they would take long walks to a chapel called Chrishona.

The Chrishona chapel, a favorite place for tourists, stood on top of a heavily wooded hilltop about five miles northeast of Riehen. In the spire was an observation platform with several large telescopes. People could view the Jung Frau and the Matterhorn, two of the better known alpine peaks in the far distance. On a clear day, the panoramic view of the Alps was breathtaking. The Kozaks usually stopped for a light snack in a nearby restaurant on their return hike home Sunday evenings, feeling rejuvenated.

They always planned to immigrate to the United States, but now time seemed vital. Their displaced person status was near expiration. They had lived in Switzerland for two and a half years, when Rose received a letter from Josephine that their mother had suffered a stroke. She had not seen her mother in over nineteen years and was very anxious to return home. Anthony sent his resume to the Ivkovich and the Kousak families, hoping they would pass it on to companies in the United States in need of his abilities. James Kousak, Rose's father, passed it on to the employment office at Chrysler Corporation in Highland Park, Michigan. Unfortunately, Chrysler was not hiring at that time. Josephine and Paul Ivkovich gave Anthony's resume to their friend and neighbor, Mr. Walter Abenroth, the owner of a lumber company. Mr. Abenroth passed it on to friends at the Parke Davis Company in Detroit, a pharmaceutical firm, which needed someone with Anthony's qualifications. A United States visa was granted to the Kozaks in the late fall of 1951.

Rose, hearing that her mother was becoming weaker, emigrated first with Jon in January 1952.

Anthony, after finishing his business projects for Transport Ltd, followed six months later with Zdenka, who by then had finished her first year at the Basel Institute of Art.

SWISS CONSULATE
competent for Bavaria with the exception of Pfalz
MUNICH
Seestraße 2

File no. D. 11.
Aktenzeichen: D. 11.

Munich, 2o. Okt. 1949 or.
Visitors' hours: between 10 and 12 a. m.
except Saturday and Sunday.

FRau Ruzena Kozakova
München

This is to inform you that I am authorized to grant you an entry-visa for Switzerland. Upon presentation of your valid passport or another official document and the necessary Exit-Permit of the Combined Travel Security Board, I will deliver the visa.

Ich beehre mich Ihnen mitzuteilen, daß ich Ihrem Gesuch um ein Einreisevisum für die Schweiz aus eigener Kompetenz zu entsprechen vermag. Für die Eintragung des Visums ist mir mit Ihrem Reisepaß oder amtlichen Lichtbildausweis das für die Auslandsreise erforderliche Exit-Permit der Militärregierung (Combined Travel Security Board) vorzulegen.

FOR THE SWISS CONSULATE:
FÜR DAS SCHWEIZERISCHE KONSULAT:

Town (or towns) to be visited: B a s e l
Ort (e):

Length of journey: Gesuch hängig
Dauer:

Reason for visiting Switzerland: Vorbereitung der Weiterreise nach USA
Grund:

entrance at:
Einreise:

Crossing the border: beliebig
Grenzübertritt:

exit-at:
Ausreise:

Last day for delivery of visa: 2o. April 195o
Letzter Visierungstag:

Remarks: gültiger tschechischer Auswanderungspass
Bemerkungen/Bedingungen:

good News for Rose, Zdenka & Jaroslav Allowing them to enter Switzerland Fee: *(from Munich refugee camp)*
Visierungsgebühr:

Good news for Rose, Zdenka, and Jaroslav,
allowing them to enter Switzerland.

140

Chapter 23

The man who goes farthest is
generally the one willing to do
and dare. The sure-thing boat never gets
far from shore.

-- Dale Carnegie

On January 12th, 1952, Rose and Jon traveled by train from Basel to Paris, where they stayed overnight in a rented room. The next day, they boarded another train to Cherbourg, a seaport in northern France on the English Channel. That night at eleven o'clock, a large skiff picked them and many other people up from the harbor pier and carried them to the *SS Neptunia,* a Greek vessel sailing from Rotterdam, via Cherbourg, to Nova Scotia and on to New York. It was a creaky, rusty, old ship on her last voyage, but because Rose was desperate to see her mother it was the fastest last-minute way to America. They were placed into a cabin below deck with four other ladies. By the time they were situated, it was past midnight, and Jon finally fell asleep, sharing a bed with his mother. The next morning, he woke up feeling very seasick. Rose quickly helped him to the women's bathroom, where she held his head over a toilet bowl while he threw up. She then hurried him topside, into the fresh sea air.

"Breathe deeply!" she commanded. The wind felt cold and harsh against his face, and spray from the waves blew over his head as he stood near the rail, looking in awe at the stormy North Atlantic.

"I'm hungry," he told Rose.

"Good," she said, thinking he was feeling better. "I'm hungry too." They walked into the dining room and noticed dishes sliding across tablecloths.

"We are in a gale," a young waiter, walking up to them, apologized. "It happens frequently this time of the year in the North Atlantic. But it is nothing to worry about. We have a good captain who has made this journey many times. The boat may rock, but it is very stable."

"We would like to eat a light breakfast please," Rose told the waiter. "I would like coffee and buttered toast and my son would like cereal."

"May I suggest a bowl of corn flakes for the young man?" asked the waiter, familiar with the signs of seasickness.

"That would be fine," replied Rose. "I hope it settles his stomach."

Breakfast was served, and Jon dug into his corn flakes.

"It's delicious," he told Rose, finishing it quickly. "I would like another bowl, please."

"In America, there are many breakfast cereals to choose from," Rose said.

"I'll have to try them all. I still like *buchermusli,* (a Swiss breakfast food), but these corn flakes taste great," Jon replied, wiping his chin, his seasickness forgotten.

That same day, Rose made arrangements for their own cabin with two beds. They both slept better with the additional privacy.

On the third day, near Greenland, they spotted icebergs in the distance. Some of the passengers became alarmed, citing the Titanic disaster years before.

"There is no need for alarm," a ship's officer explained. "We are a safe distance from the icebergs. Our captain does not take chances." This seemed to quell their fears.

In the meantime, Jon made friends with several Canadian boys his age. They were traveling back home with their families after celebrating Christmas with their grandparents in Holland. Jon and his newfound friends spent their days exploring the vessel. They watched from the pilothouse, with the captain's permission, as gigantic waves swept over the bow of the ship, at times, completely submerging it, only to see it reemerge a few moments later. The ship would slowly climb up the next mountain of water, creaking and pulling its way up, only to descend into what seemed an abyss down the other side, just barely defying the forces of nature. They were allowed to visit the crew's dining room and at times watched the crew at work. Most of the crew was Greek, but language was never a problem; big smiles and sign language sufficed. Rose wasn't worried over her son's safety, having spoken with the ship's officers and the other boys' parents; she was assured that the crew would keep an eye on them all and that the restricted areas were always locked.

On the fifth night, at 3:00 AM, everyone was awakened by a shrill alarm. A loudspeaker advised all passengers to put on their lifejackets and report topside immediately. Rose quickly dressed, put on her lifejacket, and helped Jon with his. They hurried topside with all the other frightened people and stood near their lifeboat, as ordered, shivering in the bitter cold. It was a starlit night and the ocean was calm, but there was another ship visible in the distance, which seemed to be listing to one side. Icebergs were visible but didn't appear to present a danger. A short time later, the all-clear signal was given, and everyone was asked to return to their quarters.

The next morning, Rose was told that the other ship glanced off a small, nearly submerged iceberg and was taking on water. The *Neptunia* was one of several ships within a ten-mile distance poised for a rescue. As their ship slowed, they were told that one of the two generators on their ship had stopped working, possibly necessitating an evacuation. In the meantime, anther ship that was closer to the one in trouble came to their aid. The captain of the *Neptunia* was thanked for providing support but told that no further help was needed. Apparently, when the ship's engines resumed their cruising speed, the generator started working again and all was well.

"Thank God for that," Rose said, "we don't need any more problems."

On the ninth day, they reached Halifax, Nova Scotia, Canada, during a howling snowstorm. Jon had a sad separation from his shipboard pals. Although none of them spoke Jon's languages, German or Czech, they had communicated well with sign language and would miss each other.

The next morning, it was still snowing when the *SS Neptunia* entered New York harbor. Rose and Jon were topside early, bundled up in warm clothing, cheering with hundreds of others as the Statue of Liberty came into view through the falling snow. It was an emotional moment; some people were crying, while others were on their knees on the snow-filled deck, thanking God for their safe arrival in America. Many of the passengers were refugees from the war or escapees from behind the Iron Curtain, seeking a better life in the United States.

Rose held Jon tightly with both arms as she looked at the Statue of Liberty, tears running down her cheeks. "This is the land of opportunity," she said to him. "Our family will make a new start here, and good things will happen. Thank God we finally arrived!" Nine-year-old Jon felt the intensity of his mother's words and believed her.

Chapter 24

*I look forward to … a future in which
our country will match its military strength
with our moral restraint, its wealth with our
wisdom, its power with our purpose.*

--John F. Kennedy

Rose and Jon went through immigration, a tedious five-hour process, and finally boarded a Greyhound bus bound for Detroit, Michigan, around 6:00 PM. The bus made several stops along the way. Rose and Jon tried sleeping during the night, but nervous energy kept them awake. The anticipation of seeing her parents once again and the excitement of starting a new life gave Rose much to think about. Jon nodded off a few times, only to awaken whenever the bus stopped so that he could step off and examine this new world he had heard so much about. At one stop, around 4:00 AM he asked his mother if he may buy chewing gum and how to ask for it in English. Rose told him in German (they communicated in Czech or German), "Just go up to the counter and say, 'I would like gum, please.' Gum is understood by everyone, and you should not have any trouble."

Jon repeated the words a few times, stepped off the bus, and walked into the restaurant and up to the counter. He confidently said to the smiling lady on the other side, "I would like gum please."

She looked at him and asked, "What kind?"

Confused, he repeated, "I would like gum, please."

The kind lady, understanding his dilemma, pointed to the shelf displaying many different flavors and again asked, "What kind would you like?" He didn't understand her words but her pointed finger helped. He selected a colorful orange pack and smilingly intimated that it was what he wanted. She gave it to him and said, "That will be five cents please." Not knowing U.S. currency, he gave her the quarter Rose gave him and proudly walked back to the bus.

The bus driver followed him a few minutes later and gave Rose twenty cents change, saying, "The lady at the counter didn't expect a tip from the nice young boy in knickerbockers." Rose thanked him and commented on the honesty of the clerk.

"What kind of gum did you buy?" she asked. When he proudly pulled the orange pack out of his pocket, she noticed it was clove. Not wishing to hurt his feelings, she said, "What a great choice!"

He stuck a piece in his mouth, but after chewing for a few minutes and feeling the numbness in his mouth, he decided he didn't wish to deprive his mother of such a "great choice" and gave it to her.

They arrived in Buffalo, New York, at about 10:00 AM, with enough time to walk the short distance, in the falling snow, to Niagara Falls. Rose and Jon felt very small viewing this awesome force of water cascading over a very large, horseshoe-shaped precipice surrounded by a snow-covered landscape. It was a sight they would never forget and would always marvel at with each successive visit.

Their bus crossed the Niagara River, into Canada; stopped in London, Ontario; and proceeded on to Detroit. They crossed the Ambassador Bridge from Windsor, Ontario, by 8:00 PM that evening.

Jon, sensing his mother's excitement, became very anxious himself, wondering what his new grandparents were like, where he would go to school, and how he would communicate with everyone. He remembered his mother's stories describing those wonderful department stores, JL Hudson and Sears and Roebuck, where his Aunt Josephine purchased his Cisco Kid cap guns. All these thoughts tumbled around in his mind when they stepped off the bus for the last time.

They had just made their way through customs, when, all of a sudden, a booming voice yelled, "Rosie!" Jon watched in surprise as a big, elderly man wearing a gray overcoat and a gray hat swept his mother off her feet. He gave her a huge bear hug and a big kiss on the cheek, saying, "Thank God you're home!" It was a joyful reunion in the customs house, on the Detroit side of the Ambassador Bridge, where they finally arrived on January 28th, 1952.

Rose, with tear-stained cheeks, said to Jon, "This is your grandfather Kousak." The big man, with a wide, friendly smile, picked him up, gave him a hug, and asked in Czech, "*Jak se mash, mali pan?*" (How are you, little man?) It was instant love, and Jon's fear of not being able to communicate was soon forgotten. Outside, along the curb, sat a shiny red Studebaker driven by Rose's youngest sister, Ann. More hugs, kisses, and joyful tears followed before they were finally driven to Rhode Island Street, in Highland Park, Michigan, Rose's parent's home.

Her mother, Hedwig Kousak, who was recovering from a stroke, was beside herself with joy. "Rosie, my Rosie!" she cried, tears streaming down her face. She hugged Rose tenderly, saying, "So wonderful to see you!" It had been twenty years since she last saw Rose. After more joyful crying, hugging, and remembering, Rose's parents lamented their failure to become U.S. citizens before Rose traveled abroad, and felt responsible for her problems.

"Please forgive us, Rosie. We made a terrible mistake by waiting so long before becoming U.S. citizens. We didn't comprehend how much trouble it would cause you and your family."

By now, they all realized the importance of having American citizenship. Rose vowed to never allow that to happen to her family again. She made a mental note to make arrangements for all necessary instructions for obtaining their citizenship so they could proceed as soon as Anthony and Zdenka arrived from Switzerland.

Later that evening, they discussed what to do with Jon. They decided he should live with his Aunt Josephine and Uncle Paul in Reed City, Michigan, for at least a short time. They all felt he would learn English easier in a small town environment. Rose felt sad having to leave her son, but it gave her time to look for a job in Detroit and find a place for her family to live when Anthony and Zdenka arrived. During this transition period, she stayed with her parents in Highland Park. Jon wasn't sure he would like being away from his mother, living with people he didn't know. It turned out to be one of the most rewarding episodes of his life.

Chapter 25

*What charms are there in harmony of
minds and in friendships founded on
mutual esteem and gratitude.*

--David Hume

When Aunt Ann drove them all up to Reed City, Jon was worried. During their four-hour trip up US 10, through snow-covered northern Michigan, he practiced the greeting Rose taught him. She had reminded him to smile, shake hands, and say, "How do you do?" They pulled up to the large, green and white, century-old house by 7:00 PM. He nervously followed his mother, Aunt Ann, and his grandparents through the door, ready to smile, extend his hand, and greet his new relatives. Aunt Josephine didn't give him that chance. After hugging his mother, she scooped him into her arms and said, "This must be Jon." He tried his best to say, "How do you do?" but the words got muffled in her embrace. At least he used it on Uncle Paul.

"I am fine, young man," replied Uncle Paul. He shook Jon's extended hand, pulled Jon toward him, and gave him a warm hug, saying, "Let's just dispense with all this formality; after all, we are family!"

When Jon saw how much his mother missed her sister Josephine and witnessed their loving reunion, he felt better. After all, he thought, it was Uncle Paul who saved his life by sending the penicillin in his hour of need. *How bad can they be?* He didn't have much choice in the matter, anyway, but decided to give it a chance by not making a fuss and causing undue embarrassment for his mother.

Aunt Joe; Uncle Paul; their children Stephen, Helen, and Pauly; and their boarder, Bob Lackney, gave him a warm welcome. His name was soon Americanized to John.

For a time, Reed City became his second home. One Saturday morning, Uncle Paul and John's cousin Steve took him to a men's clothing store, where he shed his knickerbockers for the last time and put on American jeans and a cowboy shirt. Since it was close to lunch time, Steve suggested to Uncle Paul, "Let's treat John to a hamburger and a malted milk at Dykama's drug store."

"It may be too rich for him," Uncle Paul replied. "European diets are less fatty."

"Don't worry. I'll eat anything he can't finish," Steve said, with a big grin. John didn't know what his uncle and cousin ordered for him but was determined to finish it to show his appreciation. He didn't get past eating half of his hamburger and a few sips of malted milk before he started feeling sick. Steve gladly finished it for him.

John was enrolled, midterm, in the third grade in a Reed City elementary school and began his American education. His very kind third grade teacher, Mrs. Blanchard, made an extra effort to help him speak English. She also noticed his knowledge of geography and history and allowed him to take both subjects with sixth graders. He never forgot her name or the kindness she bestowed on him. John made many new friends. After school, during the winter, they ice-skated and played hockey. When the weather warmed, he learned to play baseball and swam with his friends at Black or Red Bridge, two popular swimming holes on the Hersey River.

John's favorite treat was when his cousin Steve took him fishing at the various lakes and streams around Reed City. They fished above Tippy Dam for bass and walleye, on Chippewa Lake for perch and bass, and at the Hersey River for trout.

His cousin Helen let him use her blue Hiawatha bicycle, which he peddled all over town, visiting friends and sometimes taking it to fish at nearby Johnson's Creek. The family dog, an English springer spaniel named Molly, always followed him wherever he went. Aunt Josephine promised to cook anything he caught as long as he promised to eat it. At first, it sounded good, but after eating suckers, shiners, and catfish, he became more selective, only keeping perch and trout.

Living with his aunt and uncle made his assimilation much easier. With their help, his mastery of English was quick, and with his knowledge of Czech and German, he was tri-lingual. Later in life, he wished he had kept up his Czech and German.

In July, with the arrival of Anthony and Zdenka, the family made a home in Detroit, Michigan. John did not wish to leave Reed City and pleaded with his parents to let him stay.

"It's like my second home," he cried. "All my friends are here."

"It isn't fair for Aunt Josephine to have to take care of you along with her own family," Rose said. "She only did it to help us until we were all together again." John, who was now almost eleven years old, sadly understood his mother. He knew he would never forget his wonderful time in Reed City, the place where Aunt Josephine, Uncle Paul, Steve, Helen, and Pauly helped him assimilate into the American way of life.

Chapter 26

We must seek, above all, a world
of peace; a world in which people dwell
together in mutual respect and work
in mutual regard.

--John F. Kennedy

Anthony and Rose applied for citizenship in June of 1952, in Highland Park, Michigan. The Kozak family moved to their new residence on Trowbridge Street, near Woodward Avenue, in Detroit. Anthony joined the Foreign Service Department at Parke-Davis Company, where he continued his forwarding duties, translating tariff-related documents from foreign countries and helping the traffic department expedite products to countries around the world. On many occasions, he was asked to be a guide for visiting pharmacists from Poland, France, and Germany, countries whose languages he was fluent in. In his spare time, he continued writing articles in German on trade-related issues for Transport Ltd.

Rose decided to contribute to their nest egg and became an administrative assistant at the JL Hudson Company in downtown Detroit. However, being an action-oriented person, she soon tired of clerical work and transferred to commissioned sales in the women's shoe department, where she thrived. She loved her work, earning many sales awards to the chagrin of Anthony, who, with his European upbringing, felt that the husband should be the sole breadwinner while the wife stayed home, tending to the general welfare of the family. He soon realized that in this new world, it wasn't shameful to have your wife contribute to the family breadbasket. Rose did her best to soothe his pride.

"You are still the main breadwinner," she said, "with your intellect and language skills. But with a dual income, we will reach our goals faster." He grudgingly accepted her decision.

Each morning, by 7:30 AM, Rose boarded the streetcar on the corner of Trowbridge and Woodward Avenue, a main artery, and took it downtown to the JL Hudson Company. She was always in a hurry, many times running diagonally across Woodward to get to work instead of crossing at the corner, accumulating many five-dollar jaywalking tickets. Anthony chastised her, jokingly saying, "Rose, for heaven's sake, at this rate your contribution will reach diminishing returns!"

John was enrolled in the fourth grade at the Blessed Sacrament Catholic elementary school on Calvert and Woodward. Zdenka became a student at Wayne University, where she studied fine art and led a busy social life. She joined the International Institute, where she met her future husband, Fred Sellenraad, an American citizen of Dutch extraction. Zdenka later became a successful interior designer, earning many awards and making Anthony and Rose very proud of their daughter.

In June of 1957, Rose and Anthony realized their greatest aspiration. They became citizens of the United States.

CHARLES E. POTTER
MICHIGAN

RAYMOND C. ANDERSON
Administrative Assistant

United States Senate
WASHINGTON, D. C.

June 24, 1957

Mr. and Mrs. Anthony Frank Kozak
1333 Pinecrest
Ferndale, Michigan

Dear Mr. and Mrs. Kozak:

May I offer you sincere congratulations upon the
attainment of your United States citizenship.

The brilliant gifts and skills brought here by men
and women of other lands have been a major factor
in our Nation's greatness.

I wish you to know that I share your hopes for the
new life you are building here. May it bring you
success and much happiness.

As your United States Senator, I stand ready to
assist you in all matters of concern to the Federal
Government and shall welcome always your views on
issues before the Congress.

Cordially,

CHARLES E. POTTER

Citizenship letter (the culmination of a monumental effort).

They learned from firsthand experience how important and meaningful this accomplishment was, remembering the problems Rose's parents created by waiting too long to earn their citizenship. Each day, they worked hard and saved their money, knowing their goals were attainable in this land of opportunity.

With their savings, they purchased a home on Pinecrest Street, in Ferndale, Michigan. Rose transferred from the downtown Hudson's store to their new location in the Northland Shopping Center in Southfield Michigan, closer to their home. Northland was the first shopping mall in the state of Michigan.

Rose felt passionate about writing the story of their escape. She needed validation that she did the right thing. Somehow, she felt responsible for placing her family into the dire situation that necessitated their escape.

Anyone who knew the story concluded long ago that there was no other way and that Rose did what was right. She was told this by Anthony and many friends who knew of her struggle. However she was not convinced and carried the burden inside. Twice a week, after work and after she cooked supper for her family, she walked one and a half miles to Woodward Avenue and took a bus to Wayne University (years later, it became Wayne State University) in Detroit to attend an evening creative writing class. During the day, she continued to sell shoes at the JL Hudson Company in the Northland Mall, becoming their highest producer for many years until her retirement. Occasionally, she purchased Irish sweepstake tickets and hoped for the best. She never won but was a gambler at heart and enjoyed taking the chance. Each morning, she walked four blocks to the corner of 9 Mile Road and Pinecrest, where she boarded a bus to Northland.

Anthony walked two miles to the commuter train, near 9 Mile Road and Hilton Road, which he took downtown to Parke Davis. He soon realized that Americans were very mobile and that with a car he would save much time and even be able to pick up Rose from work. He enrolled in a driver's training class, learned how to drive, received his driver's license, and purchased a green, four-door 1953 Pontiac. It was their first car and another accomplishment towards their many goals.

Rose also wished to drive. One evening after dinner, she demurely asked Anthony, "Aren't you getting tired of picking me up from Northland all the time?"

"Not at all, I enjoy the drive," he replied wondering what she was suggesting

That wasn't the answer Rose was hoping for and said, "If I learned to drive, I could be home from work sooner and have dinner ready by the time you came home."

"I'm sorry, Rose, but I don't think you have the temperament for driving."

"You just don't want me to be independent!"

"Not true, Rose. There are too many rules to know when learning to drive, and you don't like to follow rules. I don't want you to have an accident. Besides, we cannot afford two cars at this time. "

"That's ridiculous," she replied hotly. "You just want me to depend on you every time I wish to go somewhere. We don't need two cars. I can learn to drive the car we have; after all, I helped pay for it."

"All right, then," Anthony relented, trying to avoid another argument. "But, first you must take driver's training and pass both the written and the driving test."

Rose quickly enrolled in a driver's training class before Anthony changed his mind. Her problem was that she disregarded stop signs and traffic lights. She felt that as long as she didn't see any traffic, she could drive through a red light. Her driver's training teacher was afraid to drive with her. He called Anthony. "Mr. Kozak, your wife is a danger to herself and anyone else who drives with her. She doesn't think traffic laws apply to her."

Anthony tried talking Rose out of driving, but it didn't work. She passed her written exam and, after switching several drivers' training teachers, she finally found a sympathetic one who passed her. She now felt ready to take the driving test with a police officer and show Anthony she could drive. When the day came, she asked Anthony to drive her to the police station and let her drive their car for her road test. Anthony refused, saying, "I will not let you drive our car until you prove you are capable of driving."

"But I drove the driver's training car well and passed."

"That was only because your teacher was afraid of driving with you any longer. He felt your driving test with a police officer would determine the final outcome."

Not to be denied, Rose called her sister Ann. "Ann, I passed my driver's training class and need to take a driving test with a police officer. Would you mind driving me to the Ferndale Police Station to take my road test?"

"Why don't you ask Anthony to drive you?" Ann asked suspiciously.

"Oh, you know how he is, always wanting control. He doesn't want anyone else to drive his car. I know that once I prove to him that I earned my driver's license, he will let me drive."

Ann was in a quandary. She was very proud of her new 1956 Ford Crown Victoria and was not happy at the prospect of letting her inexperienced older sister dive it. Rose felt her hesitation and said, "Don't worry, Annie. I'll be driving with a police officer. Your car has an automatic transmission, just like the driver's training car I drove. I studied all the rules and promise that nothing bad will happen to your car."

Ann was worried because the police officer would not have a break pedal on his side like they have in drivers' training cars. She decided to help her sister anyway and drove her to the Ferndale Police Station on 9 Mile Road, one block east of Woodward Avenue. Ann reluctantly climbed out of her car and let Rose slide behind the steering wheel. The officer came out of the station, climbed into the front seat, and introduced himself.

"I'm sure this will be easy for you, Mrs. Kozak," he said, trying to put her at ease. "You probably did this successfully many times during drivers' training."

"Oh, yes," replied Rose, ready for action.

"Let's just drive up the street for a few blocks and make a couple of turns. Then you can show me how to parallel park, and we'll call it a day. Just take it nice and easy, and you will have your permit in fifteen minutes. There is nothing to it."

Ann nervously waited inside the police station, hoping that nothing would happen to her new Crown Victoria.

Rose put the gearshift into drive and pulled away from the curb, driving west on 9 Mile Road. She drove up to the stoplight on Woodward Avenue, looked both ways for traffic and, seeing none, commenced through the red light.

Woodward Avenue had four lanes going north and four lanes going south, divided by an island at that intersection. Rose drove across all eight lanes and just missed a car heading south. Luckily, the other driver slammed on his brakes and stopped just short of slamming into her right side.

"Hey! What the devil are you doing?" the officer yelled, leaning away from the door. "I have a wife and four children who I plan to see again. Do you have a death wish? You just ran a red light, endangering me, yourself, and other drivers! What were you thinking?"

"I looked both ways," Rose replied defiantly. "I did not see any traffic, and drove through. Nobody was hurt. What did I do wrong?"

It's not that Rose didn't understand the rules; she just didn't obey them if they seemed wrong to her. Had she followed the rules in her past, she would not have been able to rescue her family from the Communists. She followed her instincts.

"You broke the law, that's what!" he replied hotly. "You ran a red light and almost got us killed. I cannot let you drive. Pull over to the curb and move away from the driver's seat." When she pulled over, he opened the door, walked around the front of the car, climbed behind the steering wheel, and drove them back to the station.

At the station, he said to Ann, "You have a beautiful car, but if you wish to keep it that way, don't let your sister drive it. She seems like a nice person, but behind the wheel, she is dangerous." Ann thanked the officer and carefully inspected her car.

Later that evening, Anthony listened to Rose telling her woeful tale.

"I don't understand what I did wrong," she sobbed, despondent over not being able to drive. "I looked both ways, did not see any traffic, and drove through. What's the use of stopping for a red light if there isn't any traffic?"

Her brinkmanship did not work this time, and he was thankful.

Chapter 27

*Happiness lies in the joy of achievement
and the thrill of creative effort.*

-- Franklin D. Roosevelt

In the summer of 1958, Anthony felt confident in his driving abilities and suggested a trip. "How would you like to vacation in the Upper Peninsula?" he asked Rose. "We will take our car, and I'll ask John to help me drive."
"What a wonderful idea," Rose replied, always looking for an adventure. "John is growing older and this will probably be our last vacation together."

John turned sixteen that year. He had received his driver's license and was aching to drive his dad's second car, a 1956 Pontiac with a V8 motor and a Mallory ignition. It was a hot car, sold to Anthony by a Pontiac Motor's engineer the year before. Anthony knew John would have preferred to stay home with his friends, but by allowing him to drive part-time, he persuaded John to come along. They alternated driving every three hours or so until they reached Mackinaw City. The Mackinaw Bridge was not yet built at that time. They boarded a car ferry and crossed the straits from Mackinaw City to St. Ignace in the Upper Peninsula. In four hours, they arrived in the city of Munising, home of the Picture Rocks natural formation. Anthony stopped at the local tourist bureau to inquire of any vacancies in nearby resorts. He was told that the Grand Isle Hotel in Munising Bay was an excellent choice. They left their car in the tourist bureau parking lot, near the dock, and ferried across to Grand Isle in the hotel's thirty-foot Chris Craft skiff.

The hotel was every bit as grand as they were told. There were large cathedral ceilings, beautiful paintings, and dark oak furniture. Rose and Anthony felt it had a European charm and decided to stay for a few days. Their room was large, with two beds and a private bathroom. They unpacked, and since it was 7:00 PM, they decided to eat a light supper in the main dining room. After dinner, they walked outside for a short stroll around the resort. It was a star-filled night. A full moon reflected off the water, illuminating a rocky shoreline. Lights from the city of Munising were visible across the bay. A warm breeze rustled through the leaves.

Rose said to Anthony and John, "I think I'll take a long walk tomorrow morning. After all that sitting in the car, the exercise will feel good."

"Why don't we all go?" asked Anthony.

"Don't worry; I'll be back before breakfast," she replied. "I just need a little solitude in the woods."

Anthony knew that Rose enjoyed long walks by herself when she had something on her mind. Sooner or later, her concerns would come out.

They walked back to the hotel and turned in for the night. Their long drive had tired them out. Rose opened the window. The cool night air and sound of water lapping against the shore lulled them to sleep.

Anthony woke up around 7:00 AM to the cacophony of chirping birds. The sun's rays penetrated their curtains. When he turned his head, he noticed that Rose was gone. John was still asleep in his own bed. Perplexed, he dressed and went downstairs to the dining room, thinking she came down for early coffee. She was nowhere to be seen. He walked outside, remembering what she said, hoping to find her exploring the grounds. There was no sight of her anywhere. He walked back into the hotel and asked the clerk in the lobby if he had seen Rose, describing her as best he could.

"I remember Mrs. Kozak from when you were checking in last night. She asked where the scenic spots were. I suggested the rocky cliffs but told her to be careful. There have been a number of accidents over the years, with people slipping on the rocks and falling. I have not seen her this morning," he replied.

John came downstairs, wondering where his parents were. When he spotted his dad, he asked, "Where is Mom?"

"I don't know," replied Anthony. "Last night she said she wanted to go for a walk this morning; so far, I have not seen her."

"You know how Mom is!" John laughed. "She's probably walking along the cliffs, working up an appetite for breakfast. Last night I heard the desk clerk describing the beauty of the cliffs to her during check in."

Anthony wished he could believe that. Since he had no choice, he decided to have breakfast with John in the main dining room. After breakfast, they made a thorough search of the hotel's premises. John walked to the west of the island, along the cliffs, while Anthony walked along the other side of the island. They returned empty-handed around 1:00 PM. They thought, she would be hungry by now and felt confident she would show up for lunch. This did not happen. Rose was nowhere to be seen. By 3:00 PM, Anthony and John were worried, thinking she may have fallen from a cliff or become lost in the woods. They consulted with the hotel management.

It was decided to send out a search party by Jeep along the few lumber trails that dissected the interior of the island. They returned several hours later without luck. A sheriff's patrol boat was called to search the perimeter of the island in case Rose fell off the cliffs surrounding the island. Evening was approaching, and by now everyone who heard of Rose's disappearance empathized with Anthony and John. All the hotel spotlights were turned on in the hope they may serve as homing beacons in the coming darkness.

Rose was a long way from the hotel and knew she was lost. She watched the sun go down in the western sky from the top of a forty-foot cliff on the far side of the island. She was exhausted, hungry, and thirsty. It had been ten hours since her early morning departure from the hotel. The banana and muffins she took with her were eaten long ago. She didn't realize the island was so large. It looked smaller from the Munising pier. She chose not to walk along the lumber trails, preferring the solitude and beauty along the cliffs. Just before twilight, she noticed a boat patrolling the island about a quarter mile off shore. She tried to wave but knew she was too far away to attract notice. By now, the lumber trails were too far away and the faint noise she had heard earlier from chainsaws and trucks was long silenced. Gazing across the bay, she noticed the glimmer of lights from the city of Munising, southeast from where she stood. With rising hope, she realized that she must have walked over at least three-quarters of the island. She remembered that the hotel pier faced the city of Munising; therefore, she concluded, the hotel must be near. The moon came out, lighting her path along the cliffs. She walked carefully, keeping a safe distance from the edge. In a short while, she saw the bright lights from the hotel shining through the trees in front of her. Anthony and John were sitting on the large porch when Rose came out of the woods.

John spotted her first. "Mom, over here!" he yelled. "Where have you been? Everyone was looking for you. They all thought you had an accident!"

"I am fine," she answered, a little out of breath.

By now, the tourists in the hotel had found out about Rose's return and treated her like a heroine. She was honored as the only person to have walked completely around the island in the history of the hotel. The next day, the hotel staff hung a plaque on the lobby wall with the following inscription:

On July 25th, 1958, Mrs. Rose Kozak from Ferndale, Michigan, walked 26.4 miles around Grand Isle.

The plaque remained on the hotel wall until the hotel burned down many years later. In the meantime, Rose received many calls congratulating her, from female tourists who visited the hotel.

Two days later, they were driving between Copper and Eagle Harbor, along the Lake Superior shoreline in the Keweenaw Peninsula. It was an unusually hot, cloudless day. The temperature hovered near ninety, and the sandy beach along the road beckoned to Rose.

She turned to Anthony and said, "Let's stop the car, take a short rest, and just enjoy the beautiful view while I take a swim to cool off." Anthony and John stepped out of the car while Rose changed into her bathing suit. Anthony took off his shoes and socks, rolled up his pant legs, and waded in up to his ankles. John skipped flat stones across the water. Rose jumped in and swam out into Lake Superior. A short time later, an older man walking his dog commented to Anthony, "You better get out of that water before you freeze your legs off."

"You worry about *my* legs?" Anthony asked, baffled. "My wife is swimming at least a quarter mile off shore!"

The man, a local, was dumbfounded. He noticed Rose swimming in the distance, a speck in the water. "Why, she'll freeze to death! I'll hurry back to my house and call an ambulance." Anthony didn't think that was necessary; however, the man insisted and ran off to his nearby home, his dog chasing after him.

An ambulance from Copper Harbor arrived twenty minutes later, just as Rose was climbing out of the water, looking blue and very cold. The paramedics tried to help her, thinking she may be suffering from hypothermia. She waved them away and, through chattering teeth, said, "Thank you, but I don't need any help. The water felt refreshing." Anthony just rolled his eyes. He apologized to the ambulance drivers while John enthusiastically climbed behind the steering wheel, knowing it was his turn to drive.

Ferndale, Michigan, 1958. Anthony, Rose, and John.

Chapter 28

*People must be taught to realize that in faith
they have a mechanism and power by which
they can actually live victorious, happy and
successful lives.*

--Norman Vincent Peale

John graduated from Ferndale High School in 1961. At his Aunt Josephine's suggestion and at his parent's insistence, he enrolled in Ferris Institute in Big Rapids, Michigan, close to Reed City, where he lived when he was younger. He was showing restless independence, like his mother had at that age. His parents were worried and hoped that Aunt Josephine would keep an eye on him. Although he enjoyed reading and always did well in all of his college prep English courses, the lure of money and independence proved too strong. After several semesters, he returned to Detroit.

John left his parent's home, moved in with a friend, and worked the night shift from 7:00 PM to 7:00 AM at Ford Motor in their heat treat department. He earned twelve dollars per hour, double time on Sundays. He worked seven days a week for eight months straight and earned lots of money. However, deep inside, he felt something missing. The money was great, but working in a factory was not something he wanted to do for life. In 1963, instead of buying a car, he used the money he earned to enroll in the Detroit Institute of Technology and earned a Bachelor of Arts degree. He taught school at St. Catherine's elementary school on Detroit's east side while working on his master's degree in history at the University of Detroit. Anthony and Rose were relieved.

On January 27th, 1967, John married Michelle Benkert in St. Paul's Catholic Church in Grosse Pointe Farms, Michigan. As children came and budget cuts were made in the parochial school system, he changed professions. He became a commissioned sales representative with the Faber-Castell Company, a drafting, writing instrument, and art supply manufacturer of German origin. By 1977, he started his own sales agency in related fields.

In 1968, Anthony and Rose, both retired by now, sold their house in Ferndale and moved to Frankenmuth, Michigan, to be near their daughter's family.

Zdenka and Fred Sellenraad lived on a forty-acre productive flower and tree farm with their children. They named their farm Klein Bloomendahl (Little Flowers) after the Dutch town near Amsterdam where Fred was born. Twenty acres were used for cultivating and growing Chrysanthemums, which they sold each fall. The other twenty acres were used for growing and selling shade trees, a joint venture with Fred's brother-in-law Lee Allen and his family. They worked the farm during their spare time after coming home from their perspective occupations: Fred was an insurance agent and Zdenka, an interior designer. Their children helped when they came home from school, and Rose and Anthony contributed whenever time permitted. It proved to be healthy outdoor work and a great stress-reliever after a day in the office.

Rose loved to cook. She remembered many of Julia's recipes. Many times she would experiment while cooking for Zdenka and Fred's kids. She knew that Zdenka remembered how Julia's dishes tasted and wanted to see how she measured up. Zdenka never complained and was happy she didn't have to cook. Whenever John and his family came to visit, she would try a different recipe. On one such occasion, she decided to cook a Czech dish called *Svickova*, which was beef tenderloin with sour cream. First, she would brown the vegetables with bacon and butter. Then she would add the meat and brown both sides. She would add one cup of water, salt, black pepper, a bay leaf, and a pinch of thyme. Michelle, John's wife, would carefully watch and try to remember what she saw, but it was to no avail. Rose never measured anything. It was always a pinch of this and a pinch of that. After dinner, Rose usually served hot apple strudel topped with a scoop of vanilla ice cream. John and his family drove back to Grosse Pointe satiated. Although Michelle was an excellent cook, she was frustrated with her inability to copy Rose's recipes.

Zdenka and Fred's kids, Patrick, Karen, Willem, and Lee, saved the money they earned selling Chrysanthemums and paid for their college tuition. Patrick graduated from Michigan State University with a degree in horticulture and become a well-known landscape designer in Mid-Michigan. He designed portions of the river walk in Frankenmuth, Michigan. Karen graduated from Delta College and followed in her mother's footsteps, becoming an interior designer. Willem graduated from Northwood Institute, in Midland, Michigan, and became a software designer. He started a company that built circuit boards used by attorneys. Lee also graduated from Northwood Institute and sold office furniture for Steelcase in Grand Rapids, Michigan. He later became self-employed designing commercial offices.

John and Michelle's kids all graduated from college. Michael graduated from Michigan State University and sold circuitry programs for Verizon. Andrew graduated from Sienna Heights University and became a registered nurse at Oakwood Hospital in Dearborn, Michigan, and is studying to be a nurse anesthetist. Keith graduated from Michigan State University, became a stock broker, and is now a vice president with Smith Barney. Cynthia, the youngest, graduated from Champlain College in Burlington, Vermont, on December 12th, 2006, with a major in English.

Rose and Anthony built a duplex in town and lived in one half while renting out the other. They tended to the upkeep of their property, helped Zdenka and Fred sell Chrysanthemums each fall, and became busy with charity work. Anthony read stories in German to the elderly in a nearby Lutheran nursing home. The residents enjoyed listening to their mother tongue. Rose was busy gardening and helping Zdenka with her children.

Rose enjoyed having her grandchildren visit for a week or two during the summer. She loved to cook for them. She knew that one of their favorite requests was *palacinky*, thin pancakes, and she made sure she had all the ingredients ready. Rose would mix eggs, salt, sugar, milk, and flour together, and beat it until smooth. She would heat a frying pan brushed with butter and would pour in a thin layer of batter, spreading it by deftly tilting the pan. The pancakes were so thin that they appeared transparent. She fried them on both sides until golden brown and served them rolled up with jam and cottage cheese inside. The aromas emanating out of her kitchen were so mouthwatering that they only intensified the boys' hunger. When the pancakes were ready, the boys attacked their food like hungry lions. Rose would cook at least thirty pancakes for her grandsons, but it was never enough. They ate them all and asked for more. She was only too happy to oblige. No one ever missed a meal at Rose's.

Chapter 29

We seek peace, knowing that peace is the
climate of freedom.

--Dwight D. Eisenhower

In the spring of 1968, Rose developed cabin fever. She read about the Prague Spring under Alexander Dubcek, the new premier of Czechoslovakia, who ousted Antonin Novotny, a Communist hardliner. She longed to show Anthony how they escaped, to take him to Modrava, to the inn where they stayed and the trail they took to the West German border. It had been nearly twenty years since their escape, but Rose still felt she needed to validate her actions to Anthony. She knew that they both loved to hike and thought that this would be an ideal opportunity to relive some of the wonderful times they had experienced, now that Czechoslovakia was at peace.

"Anthony, why don't we go to Prague?" she asked. "It looks like it would be safe to return. Dubcek is abolishing censorship and establishing favorable trade relations with the West. All the newspapers are full of stories of how the role of the Communist Party is much reduced. I'll bet that soon they will have free elections and become democratic like the United States. Why, we could visit our old home and travel to all the places we knew so well. It would be a wonderful vacation." Rose was anxious to go and threw in an incentive: "I can even show you where your mother and father are buried." She saw him look at her and heard him sigh.

"Rose, you know that I would love to go, but as long as the Communists are in power, we would not be safe, regardless of how benign they sound. Dubcek means well, but Russia controls their satellites with a tight fist. Mark my words: they will not allow Dubcek to turn Czechoslovakia into a democracy. I am afraid that if we went, they would grab us and we would never see our kids again. Let's just wait and see what develops. If by fall the situation in Prague continues to improve, I may reconsider, but at this time I must say no."

Anthony's intuition proved correct. By September of 1968, Warsaw Pact troops from Poland, East Germany, Hungary, and Bulgaria stormed into Czechoslovakia, ending Dubcek's democratization. When the Western powers objected, the Soviet Union made a big show over the occupation by sending Aleksei Kosygin, the Russian premier, to the ceremonies marking the withdrawal of the Warsaw Pact armies, attempting to show the West their peaceful intentions. However, four Russian divisions stayed in the Czech Socialist Republic until 1987. Alexander Dubcek became a low-level bureaucrat in Bratislava.

In 1980, wanderlust captured Rose once again. At the age of seventy-three she discussed with Anthony her desire to visit his ailing sister, Olga Silberbauer, in Deutschlandsberg, Austria.

"Anthony, your sister is ill and will be very happy to see someone from her direct family. I can help her," she pleaded. Anthony hurt his back and was unable to travel at that time; however, he worried over his sister's health so he agreed to Rose's trip.

It all fit into Rose's plan. She flew into Vienna, but instead of traveling to Deutschlandsberg, she took the first train to Prague. She reflected on all her past experiences and wanted to see her old home on Hrebenkach Street once again before she was too old and infirm. Unfortunately, as she was stepping off the train in Prague, she slipped and fractured her left foot. An ambulance took her to a hospital. Her foot was placed into a cast, and she was advised to stay overnight. Rose refused to stay, fearing what may happen if the Communists delved into her past and what Anthony may do if he found out. At that time, any accidents involving western tourists were reported to the STB, the police.

A cursory investigation revealed her escape in 1949, raising suspicion as to why she returned. The police came to the hospital and questioned her. An officer asked Rose, "Mrs. Kozak, why have you come to Prague?"

"I heard it was a beautiful city, and since it was a short trip from Vienna, I decided to see for myself," she replied.

"Has it changed much from 1949?" he asked, smiling.

"I don't know what you mean," she replied, her stomach knotting up, knowing how Communists fabricated information to fit their purpose. *How did they know about her escape thirty-one years ago?* she wondered. Why bring it up now? Were they planning to hold her hostage to bring Anthony back to face their made-up criminal charges from thirty-one years ago?

"Mrs. Kozak, you are an American citizen this time. We cannot detain you against your will," the police officer said, noticing her anxiety. "However, we are concerned over your injury and suggest you spend the night in our hospital."

"No, thank you," she replied nervously. "I wish to take the next train back to Vienna." The Czech authorities did not wish to be responsible for a stubborn American with a broken foot. The police summoned a taxi to take her to the train station and have her board the next train back to Vienna. She agreed, but instead of going to the train station, she asked the taxi driver to take her to Hrebenkach.

"Would you be so kind and drive by a house that I was asked to look at by friends of mine?" she asked with mock innocence. "I believe they said it was on a winding street called Hrebenkach, near Masaryk Stadium. Do you know where it is?"

"I know the general area and will take you there, madam, but you will have to point the house out," replied the driver, courteously. "Do you have the address?" he asked.

"No," she replied. "I have a good description."

They drove for fifteen minutes before the driver asked, "We are getting close. Please describe the house." He was slowing down. "We are approaching Hrebenkach"

"I was told that it was a two-story gray stucco house with two large Linden trees in front. There should be a stone staircase nearby, leading to the street below." Rose described it to the best of her memory.

They drove slowly through the tree-lined, winding streets Rose remembered so well. Suddenly, there it was.

"Please stop," she said softly. The Lindens were gone; the stucco was faded and cracked in spots, showing its age; the gutters looked rusty; and a garage was added. Nevertheless, she knew it was the right house.

The driver heard Rose sob. He looked in his rearview mirror and noticed her quickly pull a hanky out of her purse and dab tears from her eyes. He replied, "Many things have changed since October 1949, Mrs. Rose Kozak. The state has made many changes since you left. This house, for example, is home to four families. Much more equitable, don't you think?" he asked with a smile.

"I don't know what you mean," replied Rose, startled by his knowledge, realizing he was not just a cab driver.

"The state still needs to know where foreigners wish to travel, including a former Czech resident with American citizenship, Mrs. Kozak." He was with the Czech police. "Now I really must take you to the train station."

Rose was frightened, wondering if he would take her to the train station or someplace else, remembering how it used to be. She soon realized her fears were unfounded. He drove her to the station and helped her board the first train to Vienna. "My instructions are to give you these pills in case your pain returns." He gave her several strong analgesics and wished her a safe trip back.

Once the train was moving, she threw the pills out the window, still not trusting the Communists. By the time the train reached Vienna, her leg had swelled up and was throbbing. She was in severe pain and unable to walk. The conductor called an ambulance, and Rose was driven to a nearby hospital, where she was forced to stay. They cut the cast off, gave her analgesics, and repacked her leg.

She called Olga, Anthony's sister, who lived in Deuchlandsberg, Austria, a small town north of the Italian border.

"Olga, I fractured my left foot stepping off the airplane from the United States. I am in a hospital here in Vienna and will not be able to travel for a few days."

"That's terrible. I will take a train to Vienna to be with you," Olga replied.

"No, please, that will not be necessary," Rose said, frightened that Olga would find out about her trip to Prague and telephone Anthony. "I'll be well enough to travel in a few days and will take the train to Deuchlandsberg."

A few days later, Rose showed up at Olga's house on crutches, her leg in a walking cast. Instead of taking care of Olga, as was the plan and her reason for traveling to Austria, Olga took care of Rose. They convalesced together, and in a few weeks, they had both recovered.

Anthony found out the true story three years later while browsing through old bills. He found a worn train ticket from Vienna to Prague, for the dates that Rose was there. He was sitting at the dinner table, looking at the rumpled ticket, and nonchalantly asked, "Rose, did you fracture your leg in Vienna or in Prague during your trip to visit my sister Olga three years ago?"

She was knitting in a chair, watching TV, when she realized he found out. "What are you talking about?" she asked defensively.

"Isn't this your train ticket?" he asked. He stood up and placed the ticket on her lap.

Darn, she thought recognizing the ticket; *I must have misplaced it and then forgotten about it.* "It looks like my train ticket," she answered elusively. "Let me take a closer look at it." She knew she could not finagle her way out of this one and decided to come clean. "Okay, I was there," she confessed, "but I also helped your sister get well and came home safely, didn't I? Why bring this up now, after three years, since everything turned out fine?" she asked defiantly.

"Did you visit our old address in Prague?" he asked in an interested but a non-confrontational voice.

"Yes. It was a very nostalgic trip. Had you been well enough to go, you would have loved it," she replied.

"Was that where you fractured your leg?" he continued.

"Well, had you been with me, I probably would not have fractured it," she retorted.

He decided to let it go. What could he do? he mused. He married a fearless woman with adventure in her veins, a wonderful wife and mother. She took many chances, but without her courage, their successful life in the United States would not have happened.

Rose and Anthony in 1975. Frankenmuth, Michigan.

Chapter 30

*It gives me a deep, comforting
sense that things seen are temporal
and things unseen are eternal.*

-- Helen Keller

Rose developed congestive heart failure at age eighty-three. She was prescribed various medications by her doctor and was told to curb her active lifestyle. This was unacceptable to her. She always lived life to the fullest. Not wishing to become a pill-popping vegetable, she took her medication sporadically and only when Anthony, in his concern for her health, made her. Even then, she hid the pills under her tongue only to spit them out when he turned his back.

Rose gardened with a fury, cultivating a flower garden that was the envy of the neighborhood. She joined the Frankenmuth Chapter of the Republican Party and became politically active, expounding on the virtues of free enterprise and individual effort, and warned against government handouts, much to Anthony's astonishment.

"Rose, please slow down so you may watch your grandchildren grow into adulthood," he pleaded.

"Anthony, all of our dreams came true. We escaped from the Communists, became American citizens, watched our kids get educated and hold good jobs, and watched them marry wonderful spouses and give us eight beautiful grandchildren. What else could I possibly want?" she asked. "Our grandchildren have smart, enterprising parents. I'm not worried."

To quell Anthony's fear, and at her doctor's urging, she decided to show some conciliation to a more sedentary lifestyle by enrolling in an oil painting class. Her passion became painting flowers. She painted with fervor, many times, into the early morning hours. Her paintings adorn the walls of her children and grandchildren's homes.

Her last act of self-assertiveness was in the fall of 1992, on a cold Saturday afternoon. She left their house in Frankenmuth without telling Anthony, who was preoccupied in the basement with a woodcarving project. A short while later, Anthony came up for coffee. He noticed her absence and, aware of her weak heart, called Zdenka.

"Your mother left the house without telling me. It would not surprise me if she decided to walk to your place."

"That would be a five-mile walk," replied Zdenka, concerned. "She is too weak to come this far."

Nevertheless, knowing her mother, Zdenka wouldn't put it past her. Fred quickly picked up Anthony in his car, and together they scoured the town and nearby roads. It was now becoming dark, and there was still no sign of Rose. Unable to find her, they sat around Zdenka's kitchen table, wondering where she could have gone, and contemplated calling the police.

Suddenly, the side door opened, and Rose walked in thirsty and exhausted but beaming with pride. She noticed their astonished looks and asked, "What's the matter with all of you? I'm fine!"

"We checked all the roads and did not see you. Which way did you come?" asked Anthony.

"Oh, I took a shortcut through the fields," she replied with a smile.

It was her last show of bravado. Rose passed away two weeks later in September 1992. She was eighty-five. Anthony died two years later, mostly of a broken heart. He was ninety-one.

Rose picked opportunity over security, took calculated risks, and always looked forward to the challenges of life over some guaranteed existence. At work, she picked the incentive of commission sales over a guaranteed salary, knowing it was the best way for her to get ahead. Yet she had misgivings, feeling she let her parents down in her early years, and worried about all the times she deceived Anthony. Unknowingly, she redeemed herself many times over. She never took credit for any of her deeds; she was just happy that it all worked out. Although she was not born in America, she was an American in the truest sense of the word. Her courage, deeds, and the risks she took were attributes similar to those that built this great country.

About the Author

John was seven years old when he escaped from Communist Czechoslovakia with his mother and sister. Today, he is the president of J. Kozak Sales Inc., a manufacturer's representative agency in Grosse Pointe Farms, Michigan.

Rose and Anthony, 1992, just before Rose passed away.

Bibliography

Catherwood, Christopher. *Churchill's Folly.* Carroll & Graf Publishers, 2004.

Schom, Alan. *Napoleon Bonaparte.* Harper Collins, inc., 1997.

Fontaine, Andre. *Cold War: 1917–1950.* Random House, 1968.

Gerolymatos, Andre. *The Balkan Wars: Austria-Hungary Annexes Bosnia-Herzegovina.* Basic Book Publishers, 2002.
Isaac, Jeremy, and Taylor Downing. *Cold War.* Little Brown & Company Publishers. 1998.

Mazower, Mark. *The Balkans.* Weidenfeld & Nicolsen, 2000.
Otfinoski, Steven. *The Czech Republic: The Prague Spring and Its Aftermath.* Facts on File, 1997.
Time-Life, *Word War II: An Illustrated History—The Munich Conference,* September 29, 1939 and the sellout of Czechoslovakia